HOLDING FAST TO DREAMS

Children's March, Birmingham, Alabama, May 4, 1963. Freeman Hrabowski, twelve, is second from the left in this line of children being led to jail. (AP Photo/Bill Hudson)

HOLDING FAST TO DREAMS

Empowering Youth
from the Civil Rights Crusade
to STEM Achievement

FREEMAN A. HRABOWSKI III

A Simmons College/Beacon Press
Race, Education, and Democracy Series Book

BEACON PRESS

BOSTON

· Beacon Press
Boston, Massachusetts
www.beacon.org

Beacon Press books
are published under the auspices of
the Unitarian Universalist Association of Congregations.

This book is published as part of the Simmons College/Beacon Press
Race, Education, and Democracy Lecture and Book Series and
is based on lectures delivered at Simmons College in 2013.

22 21 20 19   8   (hc.)
22 21 20 19   8 7 6 5 4 3   (pbk.)

This book is printed on acid-free paper that meets the uncoated paper
ANSI/NISO specifications for permanence as revised in 1992.

Text design by Wilsted & Taylor Publishing Services

Library of Congress Cataloging-in-Publication Data

Hrabowski, Freeman A.
    Holding fast to dreams : empowering youth from the civil rights crusade to
STEM achievement / Freeman A. Hrabowski, III.
      pages cm
    Includes bibliographical references and index.
    ISBN 978-0-8070-0344-2 (hardback) — ISBN 978-0-8070-0345-9 (ebook)
    — ISBN 978-0-8070-5244-0 (paperback)
    1. African Americans—Education. 2. Minorities in science—United States.
3. Minorities in technology—United States. 4. Minorities in engineering—
United States. 5. Minorities in mathematics—United States. 6. Science—
Study and teaching (Higher)—United States. 7. Engineering—Study and
teaching (Higher)—United States. 8. Mathematics—Study and teaching—
United States. 9. Hrabowski, Freeman A. 10. Civil rights movements—
United States—History—20th century. I. Title.

    LC2717.H73 2015
    371.829'96073—dc23   2014041628

To my teachers in the Birmingham Public Schools

and

to my mentors and students

Contents

Introduction

They were crying. Our parents—perhaps a hundred or more—had come to hold an evening vigil of song and prayer for all the jailed children, and as they looked up at the walls of the detention center where we were held, they openly wept. They wept at the thought of their children in narrow, overcrowded cells; they wept out of fear for and maybe also pride in those children they held so dear; they wept, frustrated with an oppressive system whose time to go had come.

Tears streamed down our own faces as we looked back out the jailhouse windows at our mothers and fathers outside. Our emotions were raw.

The Reverend Dr. Martin Luther King Jr. stood with our parents. With his words, he comforted us all and lifted us up. His voice carried from where the crowd gathered, and we, the children sent to jail by the segregationists of

Birmingham, Alabama, listened carefully as he strengthened us, saying that what we had achieved by marching and willingly going to jail would change the lives of children not yet born.

What we children had achieved.

Changing the lives of others not yet born.

I was twelve at the time and could not yet fully grasp either Dr. King's meaning or his vision. I could not imagine that I would one day be president of a university that embraced a diverse student body of whites, African Americans, Asian Americans, Latinos, and students from a hundred or more countries. At the time, I had never even seen people of different races seated together or learning together; I had never spoken to anyone of another race.

For now, I was sitting behind bars, wondering not so much about generations to come but about my own future. When would I get out of this jail? What could I expect of the future? Would Birmingham, Alabama, the South, or America change so that someone like me, who was excited about school, could get an education and follow my dreams wherever they took me, even though I was black?

Ahead of me was a long journey through five decades, a journey from Birmingham to Baltimore, during which I worked to fulfill my dream of providing greater opportunity for high-achieving students so they could realize their potential, regardless of their backgrounds. This book is the story of that journey. It began in Birmingham, a city that was briefly and critically the epicenter of the civil rights movement in the spring and summer of 1963.

* * *

I was born in Birmingham in 1950, privileged to be born in a hospital but nonetheless consigned to the basement of that hospital, where the colored delivery room was located. That conflicted circumstance of my birth reveals much. Blacks in Birmingham in the 1950s experienced a confounding tension between opportunity and oppression.

Birmingham offered blacks a limited measure of economic opportunity. The city was known as the Pittsburgh of the South because of its iron and steel industry—a cast iron statue of Vulcan overlooks the city—and many blacks benefited from work in this industry, even if relegated to unskilled and semiskilled jobs in the iron and steel mills, often with incomes substantially less than those of whites. In 1960 there were about eleven thousand black steelworkers and twenty-two thousand white steelworkers in Jefferson County, Alabama, which includes Birmingham.[1] Indeed, these jobs gave Birmingham's black community sizable economic power. Middle-class black Birmingham had a high homeownership rate, and a wide range of Negro businesses—cleaners, shoe stores, barbershops, grocers, insurance companies, and even a pest-control company—that catered to the black community.[2] Our neighbors included many teachers and principals and some of the city's black doctors and lawyers.

I grew up in this Birmingham, in what blacks considered to be a privileged, educated, middle-class family, and we made the best of our opportunities. Both my parents worked. My mother was a teacher. My father had been a teacher for a time as well and enjoyed it, but working in the steel mills paid considerably more, so he took a job there. Indeed, my father held three jobs: as a steelworker, as a package handler at the railroad station, and as an associate at a local funeral home, where he helped grieving families.

Our deliberate focus on family, education, and hard work, along with strong churches and ministers, sustained a full life in the face of difficult circumstances. My friends and I took piano lessons, and we had an appreciation of the classical music, from Beethoven to Bach, that was played in our church alongside Negro spirituals and gospel music. Parents in our community spent much time nurturing their children and produced many from my generation who would become successful and even prominent black Americans.

Yet Birmingham was an oppressive place for blacks. In his April 1963 "Letter from Birmingham Jail," Dr. King wrote, "Birmingham is probably the most thoroughly segregated city in the United States. Its ugly record of police brutality is known in every section of this country. Its unjust treatment of Negroes in the courts is a notorious reality. There have been more unsolved bombings of Negro homes and churches in Birmingham than in any other city in this nation. These are the hard, brutal, and unbelievable facts."[3] Indeed, there were so many bombings and fires that the city was known as Bombingham, and a neighborhood near my home was called Dynamite Hill because of the violence used by whites to terrorize the black population and enforce the residential color line and the demeaning laws of segregation.[4] When we went downtown to shop, we saw no one of color in any position of power. Blacks could be treated in the hospital— but only after all the whites seeking care had been seen.

One day when I was about ten years old, my mother took me to the hospital's emergency room because I was having a severe asthma attack. As we sat in the colored waiting room, my condition worsening as time passed, my mother became increasingly frightened that I might die right there in front of her as we waited for all of the whites to be seen. Distressed, she walked into the white waiting room and asked, "Is there a Christian in here?" Shocked white faces turned to her, yet as she explained that her child was having a medical emergency that demanded immediate attention, several white women found the compassion to help convince a doctor to treat me without delay, possibly saving my life.

Given the tension between opportunity and oppression for blacks in Birmingham, this city was ready to become a flashpoint—and even a turning point—in 1963 in the arc of the civil rights movement.[5] The 1954 Supreme Court decision in *Brown v. Board of Education* had declared that "separate but equal" in education was inherently unequal and that segregated schools must be integrated with "all deliberate speed." Segregation, however, did not merely end in the wake of the court's decision. Instead, proponents of integration organized an effort to bring down segregation in the South—what we now call the modern civil rights movement—that met stiff resistance from those who defended the separation of the races. In 1963 the civil rights movement was nearly a decade old when it focused on Birmingham, combining the forces of the city's Alabama Christian Movement for Human Rights, led by the Reverend Fred Shuttlesworth, with the Southern Christian Leadership Conference, led by Dr. King, to organize a boycott of downtown stores and a series of marches on City Hall. These would eventually lead to the arrest of Dr. King in April, his "Letter from Birmingham Jail," and the Children's Crusade in May, which took many of us to jail and brought the violence of the South—images of fire hoses and dogs turned against children—to newspapers and television sets across the country. These events set the stage for the March on Washington in August, where Dr. King declared, "I have a dream," and delivered one of the most moving and important speeches our nation has heard.[6]

The events of Birmingham also moved President John F. Kennedy to support civil rights legislation that was enacted the following year, after his assassination. The Civil Rights Act of 1964, which passed Congress with bipartisan support after the longest filibuster in the history of the US Senate, generally prohibited discrimination in employment, education, and public accommodation on the basis of race, color, religion, sex, or national origin.[7] The act helped to desegregate schools, colleges, and universities, specifically authorizing the federal government to bring suit against those schools practicing discrimination (Title IV) and cutting off federal funding as punishment, if necessary (Title VI). Along with the Elementary and Secondary Education Act and the Higher Education Act of 1965, the Civil Rights Act of 1964 provided the legal and financial means to increase educational opportunity in the United States. This has been a great American success story—up to a point. Sadly, there has been a strong trend toward resegregation in our public elementary and secondary school districts since 1980.[8] And in postsecondary education, while the proportions of African Americans who enroll in and complete a postsecondary degree have increased substantially since, these rates remain significantly lower than those for whites.

When I talk with students on my campus about the 1960s—a period that occurred long before they were born—it is hard for them to grasp the real struggle, suffering, and in some instances loss of life that these events entailed, or their importance to their lives today. While some are fascinated by and deeply interested in learning about the civil rights movement, others wonder why they need to know about it at all. To them, the events of 1963 are a distant memory belonging to their parents or, more likely, their grandparents. What does it matter now? It is important for them to understand that the struggle was and continues to be about ensuring that all of our citizens are able to participate fully in our democracy, society, and economy.

Indeed, there is a strong difference between reading about historic events and experiencing them. To those of us who were there, who marched, who were the targets of the snarling dogs and fire hoses, and who went to jail, those events were—and are even today—very real. Consider the tragic events of September 11, 2001. We easily remember the shock, disbelief, grief, and fear of that moment when we first heard about what happened in New York City, Washington, and Pennsylvania, because we were, in a sense, there. Many people of my generation have similar memories about the four little girls killed in a church bombing in Birmingham in 1963 and the tragic assassinations of President John F. Kennedy and Dr. King in 1963 and 1968.

As we look back on the past, the outcomes of the civil rights movement can seem to have been both inevitable and complete to those who were not there. Those outcomes, however, were far from certain at the time. It took real struggle to bring about positive change. And the outcomes are not final—indeed, they have been and remain contested. This is an important lesson: progress is never assured, success is never final, and victories attained can be undone, particularly if we are not vigilant in sustaining them.

So we need to tell the stories, good and bad, because it is important to us today as citizens to know how we got where we are, to recognize the real struggle it took to get here, and, most important, to understand that even with the progress we have made, the journey is unfinished. We should not and cannot accept the present as "just the way things are." The present is just one stop on a journey that began long before 1963 and will continue well into the future. We must understand the arc of history and our place in it—as we did in 1963—and allow this knowledge to illuminate the path forward from here.

The fiftieth anniversary of the 1963 Children's Crusade in Birmingham provided me an opportunity for reflection, as I was invited to speak about the march and its consequences. This reflection led me to see how three stories have intertwined during the last half century to become a narrative about expanding justice and opportunity, and to identify some of the critical components in achieving both. This narrative focuses on how far we have come as a society, as well as what critical challenges remain for us to struggle with and overcome.

The first story is my own. I discuss how I walked in the Children's Crusade from the Sixteenth Street Baptist Church to the steps of Birmingham City Hall to demonstrate my wish for a better education than the one offered by segregated Birmingham. Many of the children who walked with me that day had their paths blocked by fire hoses and police dogs and so did not make it to City Hall. But most of us, in the end, faced the same fate: horrible days and nights in jail; for me, five. I discuss, from that beginning, my educational experiences and career from 1963 to the present, focusing on how I have worked with colleagues to empower youth and increase the success of diverse groups of students in higher education in general, and in science, technology, engineering, and mathematics (STEM) more specifically.

The second story is that of an institution, the University of Maryland, Baltimore County (UMBC), of which I have been president for more than two decades. In the same year as the Children's Crusade, the Maryland General Assembly passed legislation that authorized the establishment of a new university. This university, which became UMBC, was mandated to provide a strong undergraduate education, and developed into a research university that has played an important role in the economy of the greater Baltimore area. This university, unlike most of the other state colleges and universities in Maryland established before it, was not segregated at its founding. It was a university that opened its doors, from the very beginning, to students of all races and backgrounds. Thus UMBC represents a fifty-year experiment in higher education designed to see whether a "historically diverse institution" that sought to achieve inclusive excellence could be a success.

The third story, which provides the broader context, is the significant yet uneven expansion of educational and economic opportunity in America since World War II. The Servicemen's Readjustment Act of 1944 (the GI Bill), the National Defense Education Act of 1958, the Elementary and Secondary Education Act and the Higher Education Act of 1965, and the Education Amendments of 1972 have together created a framework for federal support for K–12 education and federal financial aid for postsecondary education. This aid now consists of need-based grants, guaranteed and subsidized student loans, work-study, veterans' benefits, and graduate fellowships.[9] The Civil Rights Act of 1964 was also instrumental in broadening opportunity—particularly for African Americans—in American society generally and in education. Federal aid to states and institutions is conditioned on compliance with civil rights laws.

While we are troubled by persistent achievement gaps and continuing disparities in educational access and opportunity, we can observe that high school and post-secondary completion and attainment have increased substantially over the last fifty years. We applaud an increase in high school attainment from 39 percent of blacks ages twenty-five to twenty-nine years old in 1960 to 90 percent in 2013. Similarly, we welcome increases in college attainment. While just 5 percent of blacks from twenty-five to twenty-nine had completed four years of college in 1960, one-fifth (20 percent) of blacks in that age group had completed at least a bachelor's degree in 2013. Yet gaps stubbornly persist and even widen at a time when postsecondary education is more salient to success than ever before in American society. The corresponding trend for whites was an increase from 12 percent completing at least four years of college in 1960 to 40 percent completing at least a bachelor's degree in 2013.[10] This book is focused on how we can increase the number of students from underrepresented groups who not only enter college but graduate, specifically in the natural sciences and engineering—those fields increasingly critical to our nation that also have the greatest underrepresentation.

Dreams are powerful, and in many ways this book is about creating opportunities for the fulfillment of dreams— possibilities that education creates for us. All that I am today began with my parents, teachers, and the adults in my community and church. My teachers, including my mother, who was very demanding of me, were particularly inspirational. They cultivated the best in their young people. They used their own money to buy supplies that students needed, and they stayed hours after school to meet with students and parents, even making home visits if necessary. They often cared for other people's children as if they were their own. My mother would take extra food to school because she knew there were students in her class who would be hungry. So, it is to the black teachers in the "colored schools" in the Birmingham public school system that this book is dedicated—because they understood our dreams and worked to make them come true. And it is their work that we must continue.

I

Standing Up for Justice

DREAMS

During college, my mother was introduced to the writing of Zora Neale Hurston, who became one of her heroes, and later mine. From Hurston, whose prose often sounded like poetry to me, I learned about two types of people in our society: people whose dreams become reality and people whose dreams are, in the words of Langston Hughes, forever deferred. Hurston's 1937 book, *Their Eyes Were Watching God*, begins, "Ships at a distance have every man's wish onboard. For some, they come in with the tide. For others, they sail forever on the horizon, never out of sight, never landing until the watcher turns his head away in resignation, his dreams mocked to death by time. That is the life of men."[1] Later in life I realized that my parents had imparted to me a key insight about these two groups of people: the difference between people whose dreams are fulfilled and those whose dreams are deferred is so often determined by education. Where would you or I be were it not for the education we each received?

Two of my own heroes growing up were Booker T. Washington and W. E. B. Du Bois. While history has positioned these leaders as antagonists, each understood the critical role of education in expanding opportunities for African Americans, thereby realizing dreams for individuals and for the race. Du Bois, born in 1868 in Massachusetts and considered by many to be the greatest black thought leader of the twentieth century, saw education as transformative for the black community. A graduate of Fisk University, he went on in 1895 to become the first African American to receive a PhD from Harvard.[2] I have always related to his notion that the highest achievers could be models for others. In his 1903 treatise, "The Talented Tenth," he wrote,

> Can the masses of the Negro people be in any possible way more quickly raised than by the effort and example of this aristocracy of talent and character? . . . The Talented Tenth rises and pulls all that are worth the saving up . . . This is the history of human progress . . .
>
> How then shall the leaders of a struggling people be trained and the hands of the risen few strengthened? There can be but one answer: The best and most capable of their youth must be schooled in the colleges and universities of the land . . . A university is a human invention for the transmission of knowledge and culture from generation to generation, through the training of quick minds and pure hearts, and for this work no other human invention will suffice.[3]

Critics have argued that this view of education and change is elitist and ignores the plight of the less fortunate in the African American community. I suggest we think of the "talented tenth" as a symbolic notion, without the numerical limit, to provide a more inclusive way to clarify the point. Just as children aspire to be the best athletes, we should be inspiring children to want to be the best thinkers and leaders.

Booker Taliaferro Washington also saw education as powerful. Born into slavery in the 1850s on a small Virginia farm, Washington moved with his family after the Civil War to Malden, West Virginia, where he worked with his stepfather in the local salt factory. Washington started learning the alphabet from a spelling book given to him by his mother, and went on to receive reading lessons from a local teacher. He later attended school, at first between shifts at the salt factory and then while working as a houseboy. He excelled as a student, eventually graduating from Hampton Institute, my beloved alma mater. Later, he became founding principal of the Tuskegee Normal Institute—now Tuskegee University—where he put into practice his vision of providing blacks with the skills and education they needed to raise up the race.[4] By the turn of the century, he had become one of the most powerful African Americans in the country, dramatically evident when, in 1901, he became the first black man to ever sit for dinner at the White House with a president.[5]

While establishing and leading Tuskegee as principal, Mr. Washington also traveled the country by train or on horseback to raise money for the institution and to talk with people of color about the importance of

education, which he facilitated by making teacher education a primary focus at Tuskegee.[6] Two of the Alabama
towns Washington visited during the first decade of the
twentieth century were Wetumpka and Selma, north and
west, respectively, of Montgomery. In each of those cities
there was a young woman in the audience who, like many
others, was so taken by what Washington said that she
began to live her life with the goal of following his advice
when she had children. His advice? Send your children to
school. Education transforms lives. The women? My two
grandmothers.

My mother grew up in Wetumpka in the 1920s and
1930s, and it was during that time she learned the pleasure of reading. Times were very hard, and to help her
family she started working when she was about twelve.
She was given the choice of being employed either as a
field hand in a hot cotton field or as a child maid in the
home of a wealthy white family. She chose the latter,
because she wanted to see how rich people lived. Later
she would observe that one distinguishing characteristic
of the wealthy was that they read a lot, which she decided she would do as well. There was no public library in
Wetumka for children of color, and the only book in my
mother's home, a wonderful book, was the Bible. Maybe
the teacher at her school had a book, but this was the
1930s and there were very few books even in schools.
The family she worked for, however, had a library in
their home, and the woman my mother worked for was
kind enough to say, "When you finish your work, Maggie, you can go into the library and read." And Mother

would do just that and become immersed in one of these books. Then the woman she worked for would tell her to take the book home and bring it back when she had finished it.

Thus she learned the importance of reading, and then of teaching others to read. In my mother's neighborhood, her girlfriends would often say, "Maggie, come on outside and play," and became upset at her when she preferred to read instead. "Why would you want to keep your nose in that book?" they would ask. It was at that point that my mother began to understand this growing difference between her girlfriends and herself. The more she read, the better a reader she became, and the better a reader she became, the more she enjoyed the experience. It was a way of putting poverty in perspective and dreaming about the possibilities. As she grew as a reader, she looked at her friends and realized the problem was this: they never read enough to get good at it, and as a result they found reading painful. She would watch them reading, frowning, using their lips, and finally they would push the book aside and say, "That's not interesting." But it was interesting, and books opened windows on the world and opportunities for those who were educated.

It was at that point that my mother discovered what she wanted to do for the rest of her life: to be a teacher. Her experience made her effective as an eighth-grade teacher specializing in English, and it shaped the way she taught me to think about reading and books. My mother often said that reading helps students learn to speak well, write clearly, think critically, and develop a sense of self. Later on, she expanded her areas of instruction. In the 1960s, when the Soviet Union launched the Sputnik satellite and Americans feared their children were falling behind in math and science, the "new math" was developed as an effort to move beyond simple arithmetic and focus on mathematical concepts and learning through discovery. Reformers developed new curricula designed to help students understand mathematical logic, set theory, and algebraic structures, placing less emphasis on basic computation. Many teachers were afraid to go back to school to learn the material, but my mother courageously volunteered for professional development to become a math teacher. I was her obliging guinea pig as she experimented with the new math and how to teach it. At that time, the things I liked most in the world were math and food; heaven for me was eating my grandmother's blueberry pie and doing math problems—getting fatter and smarter all the while. (And southerners like a child's chubby cheeks.)

Most important, my mother grasped the important relationship between language skills and solving math word problems and what that means for applying our skills in the world. The key point here is that many science and engineering problems involving health care, the environment, transportation, defense, or intelligence are not expressed in numbers but, rather, in words. Our challenge is to understand the meaning of and relationships between the words so that we can use symbols and equations to represent those relationships. The better one reads and thinks, the more clearly one understands logic—and the more proficient one becomes in solving word problems in chemistry, physics, and mathematics.

. . .

My great-grandfather, Tom Hrabowski, was a slave, the son of a plantation owner. He had several children, one of whom was my grandfather, who was named Freeman, as he was in the first generation born after slavery. Freeman owned a farm in Lowndes County, outside Selma, and that was where my father, Freeman Hrabowski Jr., grew up, working hard with his father on the farm but also working hard in his rural high school, where he, like my mother, was valedictorian of his class. Eventually, my father and his family came to one of those pivotal moments where destiny hung in the balance. My father longed to go on to college, but my grandfather told him, "You can't go, because I can't find someone to handle the other plow." My grandmother, Frances, intervened, insisting, "Our son has to go to college." When my grandfather asked who would handle the mule and the plow, she—at five feet tall—replied, "I will." And so my father went to college. And every day that my father was there he would look out the window and think about his little mother breaking her back in the hot sun so that her son could go to college. He would ask himself, "How dare I not do my best?"

My mother and father met and got to know each other in 1936 at State Teachers College, now Alabama State University, one of more than a hundred public and private historically black colleges and universities established, mainly after the Civil War in the South, to provide higher education for blacks. My father had just returned to the college after working for a few years as a teacher; at that time, you could be a teacher after high school graduation and some college. My mother had just transferred there from Alabama's State Agricultural and Mechanical Institute for Negroes—now Alabama Agricultural and Mechanical University (Alabama A&M)—which was a two-year institution at the time. My mother later told me, "When I saw your daddy I thought he was a Greek god." She'd tease me, "Boy, you look okay, but you'll never be as good-looking as your daddy." And my father then said, "Boy, when I saw your mother she was sunshine, just sunshine." After getting married in 1940, my parents worked as teachers for a time in smaller, rural school systems outside Birmingham. In 1947 they moved to Birmingham, found jobs, and built a home there. I was born three years later and named Freeman A. Hrabowski III. Later, my parents adopted my cousin, Paul, who was about fifteen months older than I but was in the same grade. We grew up together like brothers.

Both of my parents always worked very hard. My dad's degree was in education, but as it was difficult to make much money as a teacher in those days, he eventually went to work in the steel mills in Birmingham. Behind the scenes, he helped his white supervisor to read and write. At the same time, he worked at the railroad, again supporting his white supervisor in reading and writing. He also worked with grieving families at a funeral home, and helped his widowed mother supervise the farm in Lowndes County. My mother, meanwhile, became a schoolteacher in the Birmingham public schools.

My parents eventually learned from each other that their mothers had each heard Booker T. Washington speak about the importance of education all those years ago, and they realized that their lives had been affected by the impact of Mr. Washington's words. They both had been educated and had worked as teachers. They had sought a high-quality education for me, considering the importance of my education to be second only to my spiritual and character development. Throughout my childhood, I heard them discuss children's attitudes, their verbal skills, and the importance of education.

Like Washington and Du Bois, my parents were "race people," meaning they consciously worked to uplift the black race, and they believed in quality education for blacks. In the 1930s, only 3 to 4 percent of African Americans had a college education, a fact that remained true until the 1960s. Many African Americans who attended college became teachers, and often did so to become the leaders of their race. During the Birmingham bus boycotts of the 1950s, my parents gave rides to people who didn't have cars.[7] My mother also was proud to have been fired from a school system outside Birmingham in the late 1940s for trying to organize black teachers to demand salaries equal to those received by white teachers. She was such an excellent teacher that she was quickly hired by the director of colored schools in the more prestigious school system, Birmingham City Schools, where she taught until she retired in 1977.

COMMUNITY

In 1960 Birmingham was about 40 percent black and 60 percent white, with the city's 135,000 blacks living in segregated residential neighborhoods.[8] The Birmingham neighborhood where my parents and I lived, Titusville, was a very tight-knit middle-class community. My parents and many of our neighbors were constantly helping out, providing marriage counseling to struggling couples and pushing families to send their children to college. My father was very good at providing advice to other men, and he helped many to pass their General Educational Development (GED) tests. At the steel mill, he wrote articles for the Negro section of the company bulletin. While he did not believe it wise to openly address issues of unfairness, he used the articles to provide advice for men trying to support their families about the need to work hard and be their best.

Many of the families in Titusville were quite privileged relative to most black families in America, typically with both husbands and wives working. The relative economic strength and diversity of the black community were greater than the wider society may have expected. People who lived there came from a variety of backgrounds. Some had degrees from college or even graduate school, and there were a few lawyers and physicians. Though teachers in the black schools were not paid very well, they made a decent living and were better off than most. Many women teachers had husbands who worked in the steel mills. There were other people who worked for wealthy whites. They may not have had a college education, but they were broadly exposed to the larger culture and often quite polished, traveling at times with their employers outside the state and sometimes internationally. It seemed we children were always in church, participating in the youth fellowship, the Baptist Training Unit, the choir, Bible school, or going on trips. Church was just a part of life in our family and community. As children, we weren't excited about being there, but it was expected, and my church had great role models and strong families, with husbands and wives supporting each other and their children.

My pastor, beginning when I was twelve, was John T. Porter. He was an incredible human being and a remarkable pastor. A favorite son of the black community, he had left Birmingham to attend college, and he returned in his early thirties to lead our church, Sixth Avenue Baptist. He and his wife, Dorothy Porter, had graduate degrees, his in divinity and hers in music. The church itself had a number of well-educated musicians, and the music ranged from classical to Negro spirituals. For me, one of the great things about our church was that we discussed ideas and books. From Sunday school to the youth fellowship, we talked about fundamental questions. What should a human being expect out of life? What does and should American democracy mean for Negroes?

Many of us began taking piano and playing other instruments at an early age as part of our overall education. I started taking piano lessons as a four-year-old and did so for nine years. I took up clarinet in the third grade, continuing for five years in the school band. These experiences taught me a great deal about the importance of reading notes, practicing, and learning to play with others. Perhaps most importantly, they helped me to develop the confidence that practice—focusing time and attention on a piece of music—would eventually allow me to play the piece comfortably, however challenging or inaccessible it might have seemed at first. Reading a poem or solving a math problem often presented the same challenge: though the meaning or solution might at first seem remote, devoting time and attention to intellectual endeavors usually leads to greater understanding. People learn by doing, whether reading, working on math problems, or playing an instrument. Such experiences build confidence and give students different ways of thinking about the world and about themselves.

I enjoyed music, but I started loving math more and more as I grew older. I was convinced that it was not possible to excel at both, so I reached an agreement with my parents that I would stop taking piano lessons when I could play the first movement of Beethoven's *Sonata Pathétique*. I practiced that piece at a friend's house while my parents thought I was preparing to play Beethoven's *Moonlight Sonata*, a simpler piece, at an upcoming concert. I then played the *Pathétique* instead, and they were shocked. The next week, my mother was ready to take me to my piano lesson when I reminded her of our agreement. I dropped piano then, though my mother kept saying I could become proficient in both.

Did I play the *Pathétique* well? Not really. I was fairly competent. I was mistaken in thinking that because I loved math, I shouldn't be excited about music, and my parents' insistence that I continue should have told me something, but at thirteen I was just old enough to rebel. Years later, in my thirties, I went back and took lessons for several years while I was on the board at Baltimore's Peabody Preparatory, a school for the performing arts, and I came to appreciate my foundation in classical piano. What did I learn from those early years of study? I came to appreciate music from other centuries. I studied composers and their process of creating beauty. I learned a great deal about discipline and developed an appreciation for precision and subtlety. And most importantly, even at age twelve or thirteen, I knew enough to recognize who could play well and to appreciate listening. I came to understand just how hard one has to practice in order to become really good. Today, I often enjoy playing a short Chopin nocturne and find myself elevated by the music, even though my playing is, quite frankly, mediocre at best. When I give lectures, I often quote the journalist Robert MacNeil, who wrote in his memoir about the role that musical experiences played in deepening his love of language. "Music heard early in life lays down a rich bed of memories against which you evaluate and absorb music encountered later. Each layer adds to the richness of your musical experience . . . It is so with words and word patterns. They accumulate in layers, and as the layers thicken, they govern all use and appreciation of language thenceforth."[9]

CONFLICTING MESSAGES

I am convinced that our early experiences—from school, to church, to piano lessons, to shopping downtown—shape the way we think about the world and lay the emotional groundwork for decisions we will make later in life.[10] Much of my philosophy about educating students and supporting children was shaped by the messages I received and the experiences I had growing up in Birmingham at the height of the civil rights movement. The messages and experiences were conflicting, but as I witnessed and participated in events that sought to resolve these conflicts, I learned that a higher purpose, clear goals, and determination could make a difference.

My students often ask me, "Doc, what was it like to be

twelve and black in Birmingham?" I tell them that I was privileged to be born into a middle-class African American family with educated parents who provided me with strong positive messages. In the close-knit community in which we lived, everybody was my parent, and teachers gave us the best they could. It was a community that shared an understanding of the importance of education, strong faith, the arts, and reading, and of values such as hard work, integrity, and respect for others. The church was at the center of our lives. Adults looked after other children as they did their own, teaching us to be accountable and respectful. Within the sphere of this community, children were protected and made to feel special. We children were surrounded by leaders, both from within our community and beyond it, who used their language skills to shape a vision of the future. They encouraged people to believe that the world could be better than it was and that all people—including children—could be empowered to change their circumstances.

As black children living in the segregated South, however, we were subjected to another, harsher set of messages that told us we were second-class. I first became aware of these messages in 1955, when Rosa Parks was arrested for refusing a bus driver's demand that she give up her seat to a white person. I was five years old. I received the message again in second grade when the teacher handed out books with brown paper concealing the covers. Our teacher told us not to remove the paper cover but, overtaken by curiosity, I peeled it back and discovered the name of a white school underneath. I went to her and asked, "Why do they give us their books when they throw them away?" The first thing she said was, "Boy, I told you not to peel that paper off that book." Then she was embarrassed. She looked at me and said, "Yes, the book is second-rate, but you are a child of God. You're first-rate. Get the knowledge. You don't have time to be a victim." At home, I could see the pain in my parents' faces when I told them what had happened. Their message, however, was the same as my teacher's. "You have to get over it," they said. Focus on the things you can change. The messages we received from outside our community were increasingly painful as the years went on, but they taught important lessons about resilience and the value of hard work.

Segregated Birmingham told us quite clearly that we were not as good as the other children, that we were not as smart, that we did not deserve to go to the better-resourced schools. Throughout my childhood, we would go downtown, but we never saw a person of color in any position of power, not even operating a cash register. The fact that no salesperson, no fireman, no policeman, no one of authority in downtown Birmingham was of color sent strong messages to black children like me. There was a local amusement park, Kiddie Land, but we were not allowed to go there because it was for whites only. When we went to the movies, we had to sit in the balcony. At restaurants, we had to sit in certain areas or take our meals with us. In stores, we could be served but only after all of the whites in line had been. We went to separate schools that lacked the resources of white schools. It was devastating.

The same mixed messages came to us over the airwaves as well. One of the only television shows about people of color at the time was the *Amos 'n Andy Show*.[11]

As offensive as it was in many ways, we were proud to see black people on TV. Today, I am shocked by what I see when I watch that show, but that was our show—quite frankly, it's hard to explain to someone who was not there. The first regular television show that I remember as a source of real pride was *Julia* in the late 1960s. *Julia* was about an attractive, polished black nurse—played by Diahann Carroll—and her son, and it was the first time I'd ever seen a person of color portrayed with dignity on television.

Television also brought us real-life news of experiences of blacks. During that same period, the University of Alabama was under court order to open its doors to people who looked like me, with three top students from our schools—James Hood, Vivian Malone Jones, and Dave McGlathery—matriculating there for the first time. We were all so excited to watch this on television, and then we saw all these white citizens—churchgoers, I'm sure—angrily protesting the admission of blacks to the university. Soon afterwards, the governor of Alabama, George Wallace, appeared on national television, symbolically blocking the doorway of a University of Alabama auditorium to prevent the first black students from registering for classes. Under federal protection, the students registered at the university later in the day, but I remember watching the news and feeling really bad that people did not want these black students at the university.[12] I will never forget how saddened we were to be given the message yet again that we were considered second-class.

Yet the message my friends and I kept hearing from our parents, neighbors, and teachers was that we didn't have time to be victims. "You are special," they would say.

"You have to be twice as good, but if you get the knowledge, you can shape your future. Remember that you are not in this just for yourself but to change things for everyone." These were consistent and persistent messages and ones that I later incorporated into my work: people have a right to an education, and our students must be educated to become leaders, solve problems, and create better lives for others.

THE CHILDREN'S CRUSADE

From the 1930s to the 1950s, the National Association for the Advancement of Colored People (NAACP) developed and implemented a successful strategy designed to challenge the legal basis for segregation of the races in the United States. Led by Charles Houston, the NAACP legal team initiated a series of lawsuits that undermined and eventually overturned the doctrine of "separate but equal" that the Supreme Court had used to uphold segregation in its 1896 *Plessy v. Ferguson* decision. In their first case, *Murray v. Pearson* (1935), Houston and Thurgood Marshall chipped away at separate but equal by successfully arguing in Maryland courts for the admission of a black man to the University of Maryland School of Law, on the ground that the state of Maryland had no separate law school for blacks. They continued by taking further cases through the legal system all the way to the Supreme Court, with more decisions that undermined the legal rationale for segregation. In deciding *Sweatt v. Painter* (1950) and *McLaurin v. Oklahoma State Regents* (1950), for example, the Supreme Court did not overturn *Plessy* outright but did rule that separate but equal in education had to be equal in fact or it was unconstitutional. Four years later, presenting evidence that segregated schools inflicted harm on black students, the NAACP legal team, now led by Marshall, persuaded the court to finally overturn *Plessy*, and the separate-but-equal doctrine, in *Brown v. Board of Education* (1954). Earl Warren, speaking for the court, said, "We conclude, unanimously, that in the field of public education the doctrine of 'separate but equal' has no place. Separate educational facilities are inherently unequal."[13]

Following the *Brown* decision, the modern civil rights movement emerged to ensure that desegregation became a reality. It was still struggling a decade later in the early 1960s, however, to integrate public facilities and schools and ensure the rights of blacks as citizens, as many whites across the South actively resisted desegregation efforts. There was progress, to be sure. The Montgomery bus boycott of 1955–56 that followed Rosa Parks's courageous act of civil disobedience led to the desegregation of buses in that city. The student sit-in at a segregated lunch counter in Greensboro, North Carolina, in 1960 succeeded in integrating that establishment and inspiring many other students to use sit-ins across the South to win desegregation of more businesses and facilities. Though it required federal troops in each instance, black students were admitted to Little Rock High School in Arkansas in 1957 and to the University of Mississippi in 1962. Despite these gains, there were also many cities and states that continued to uphold segregation and deny voter rights. And there were many segregationists who were willing to use violence to maintain the status quo. Freedom Riders who challenged segregation in interstate transportation (buses and trains), for example, were violently attacked, and several buses set on fire.[14]

Progress toward ending segregation was uncertain and contested, resulting in occasional setbacks. In 1962 Dr. King and the Southern Christian Leadership Conference (SCLC) joined the Student Nonviolent Coordinating Committee (SNCC) and others in an effort to broadly desegregate Albany, Georgia, through nonviolent marches and other tactics. After months of protests, however, little had been accomplished. The goals of the movement were too broad, protest marches had little leverage over local white elected officials who did not need black votes, and those same officials who had agreed with Dr. King to negotiate with local blacks reneged on their promises once King left town. In addition, a federal judge granted local officials an injunction to block further civil rights marches, leaving Dr. King and the civil rights leadership who had joined the movement there with what seemed an insurmountable roadblock. The quandary was this: for King and his colleagues, protest marches were their prime tactic in Albany, and giving them up would significantly reduce their ability to apply any pressure on the establishment that supported segregation; at the same time, defying the federal court injunction, which they believed rested on shaky legal ground, would have appeared to contradict their purpose, which was to support and force the implementation in the South of federal court decisions, particularly those requiring desegregation. King and the other leaders learned about the injunction on a Saturday morning, and they decided after much deliberation not to join in a march scheduled for later in the day. The march proceeded without them to little effect, and the SCLC effort in Albany soon faltered. While some have argued that Albany was a limited success (civil rights activists learned much about goals and tactics, and Albany did desegregate a year later), King and his SCLC colleagues left the city dejected and pondering how they might proceed differently in the future.[15]

In 1963 the SCLC leadership agreed to focus their efforts on Birmingham, Alabama, my hometown.[16] The Reverend Fred Shuttlesworth, director of the Alabama Christian Movement for Human Rights (ACMHR) and one of the founders of the SCLC, had been working to end segregation and promote civil rights in Birmingham since the mid-1950s, often against violent opposition. His own home, adjacent to the Bethel Baptist Church, had been bombed in 1956. The next year, 1957, a white mob violently attacked him and his wife when they tried to register their children at all-white Phillips High School in Birmingham. In early 1963, when I was twelve, Shuttlesworth persuaded his SCLC colleagues that their next target should be Birmingham, because it represented segregation at its most intractable and could be used as a platform to raise national consciousness about the struggle for civil rights.[17]

Determined to bounce back from Albany, the SCLC leadership adopted a new, more targeted and assertive strategy for challenging segregation in Birmingham, which they eventually called Project C (the C stood for *confrontation*). As Taylor Branch relates in *Parting the Waters*, the plan of action was initially conceived as involving four stages: "First, they would launch small-scale sit-ins to draw attention to their desegregation platform, while building strength through nightly mass meetings.

Second, they would organize a generalized boycott of the downtown business section and move to slightly larger demonstrations. Third, they would move up to mass marches both to enforce the boycott and to fill the jails. Finally, if necessary, they would call on outsiders to descend on Birmingham from across the country . . . to cripple the city under the combined pressure of publicity, economic boycott, and the burden of overflowing jails."[18] While there has been scholarly discussion as to whether plans for Birmingham were actually this well thought out ahead of time, and the historical record shows that the SCLC leadership changed plans and tactics in the spring of 1963 as the political situation and protests in Birmingham evolved, the essential thrust of the campaign in Birmingham as it played out would be an economic boycott, complemented by sit-ins and protest marches. The latter eventually became the main show, escalating into a critical mass march called the Children's Crusade.[19]

The SCLC leadership hoped that these actions would force the city and its business community to reassess the costs of segregation. As the black community in Birmingham had much more economic power than in Albany, Georgia, the SCLC had determined that the boycott strategy would hit the business community hard. As Martin Luther King argued, "The Negro has enough buying power in Birmingham to make a difference between profit and loss in any business. This was not true in Albany."[20] The SCLC also bet, as Diane McWhorter has put it, that "huge, jail-filling, history-making demonstrations, during the symbolically freighted Easter season" would produce a concrete victory in Birmingham.[21] Indeed, the decision to focus on Birmingham would accomplish that and more—it would prove to be a turning point in the civil rights movement and, unbeknownst to me at the time, in my life as well.

As a child I had become painfully aware that while downtown stores in Birmingham would sell to my family and other blacks, those stores had segregated and inferior facilities for us—fitting rooms, restrooms, drinking fountains, and lunch counters. Moreover, we saw no people of color holding any positions other than janitors and maids; all of the positions from sales clerk to manager were reserved for whites. Given this treatment, the black community in Birmingham did respond to SCLC's call to boycott downtown stores. Indeed, I will never forget how depressed my friends and I were that Easter Sunday morning. Traditionally, the Easter season was the time when you could shop and get new clothes. But my parents supported the boycott, and it was a very powerful opportunity for children to understand important lessons regarding right and wrong, the power of community resolve behind a common goal, and the virtue of peaceful protest. So we kids did not get our new outfits and shoes. More than anything, we learned that sometimes, in order to achieve a long-term goal, you must sacrifice something that seems important in the short term. For us children, that lesson would very soon be put to a much more challenging test.

During April, while the boycott continued, hundreds of people were arrested in Birmingham as they participated in sit-ins and protests. As in Albany, city officials in Birmingham asked the courts for an injunction against protests and one was granted. In this case, however, after discussion and prayer, Dr. King decided to continue to protest in defiance of the injunction, which, fortuitously, had been issued by a segregationist state court and not a federal court as had been the case in Albany. On Good Friday, April 12, Dr. King and about forty others marched from the Sixteenth Street Baptist Church along a route lined with supporters. Within several blocks of the church, they and a handful of bystanders were arrested and taken to jail. A group of local white clergy wrote a letter condemning Dr. King as an "outsider" and the marches as "unwise and untimely."[22] In response, Dr. King wrote the "Letter from Birmingham Jail" that defended nonviolent resistance to racism and argued there was a moral responsibility to defy unjust laws.

Yet despite the continued business boycott and the Good Friday arrests, the number of marchers needed to pressure the white establishment in Birmingham into negotiations had not fully materialized in April. Indeed, organizers became concerned late that month that what pressure they had brought to bear was dissipating. SCLC leader James Bevel then suggested that, in order to sustain momentum, the group should call on the city's children to join the marches. Bevel noted that many adults feared losing jobs or mortgages if they joined in the protests, and so stayed home. He argued that the city's children, by contrast, were less worried about such concerns and might be recruited to keep the marches going. Moreover, as Juan Williams relates in *Eyes on the Prize*, Bevel told King that "the sight of young children being hauled off to jail would dramatically stir the nation's conscience."[23]

It was at this time that my parents brought me to church in the middle of the week for a mass meeting on the civil rights demonstrations now under way in Birmingham. I had not wanted to come along and did not want to be there. My parents placated me by allowing me to do my math homework in the back of the room, where I sang along, ate M&Ms, and worked on my algebra problems. I tried to ignore the speeches from the front of the church, but at one point one of the speakers caught my attention and held it. We were accustomed at our church to impressive speakers, but this man combined polish with a message I could not ignore. We knew that blacks were not treated fairly by those in power, but we tended to think, "This is the way of the world." In contrast, this man was saying that the world could change and that even the children could have an impact on what might happen to us in the future. In fact, he was saying that our actions were needed and mattered. I was impressed. I asked my parents, "Who is that man?" It was the Reverend Dr. Martin Luther King Jr.

It can be transformational for anyone—and especially for a child—to come to the belief that the world can be a different place from what it is right now, that the future is not decided. Many slaves may have had this experience when they heard Harriet Tubman say, "There is a railroad here. There is a way to freedom." Your dreams change, your possibilities change, your goals change.

When we arrived home after that meeting, I said, "I must go. I must go." And my parents said, "Absolutely not. You cannot go." I was stunned. "The minister that you made me come and listen to told me what I need to do, and we all gave him a standing ovation. Now we get home and I say I want to do what he says, and you tell me I can't?" Now, at that time you did not talk back to your parents. Yet I said, "You know, you guys are really hypocrites." The air was just sucked out of the room. My mother gasped, and my dad simply said, "Boy, go to your room." I was convinced I was going to be punished.

But they did not come into my room that night. They came in early the next morning and sat on both sides of my bed. I was frightened, seeing that they had both been crying—I had almost never seen my parents cry. They said, "It was not because of a lack of confidence in you that we were saying no, but you are our only son; you are our treasure. We don't trust the people in those jails. We don't know what they would do to you. So, don't think we don't believe in you. We are worried because we love you." What they said next was so powerful: "But we have prayed all night, and we are going to put you in God's hands. If you want to go, you can."

I did not know as we prepared for the march that teachers had gotten the message from the Board of Education that if their own children went to jail, they would lose their jobs. This had made it even more difficult for my mother. For several reasons, most of the children who joined the march were not from middle-class families. First, many middle-class parents were worried because they had more to lose, and many were not willing to risk jobs, mortgages, and more. Some were not happy with Dr. King. He was rocking the boat. Blacks in Birmingham had a very high rate of homeownership because of the relatively high wages earned by teachers and steelworkers. And when you've got something, you worry about losing it. Families and kids in the housing projects may have felt they had less to lose from participating. Second, many of my teachers understandably felt that the role of children was to excel in school, and that participating in demonstrations would take away from school time. Finally, and most important, most did not trust the jail staff with their children.

But I was going to march. At first I was excited, but then I began to think more about what participating in the march would be like, and I got really scared and started to cry. I had done all my big talking, to be sure, and yet I had already heard about the dogs and the fire hoses. I was not a brave child really. If there was a fight, I ran the other way. I was a chubby little math nerd. Give me a math problem to attack and I am fine. But fight another kid? I'm not fighting anybody. Face dogs and fire hoses? Really?

I tell my students that sometimes when people do courageous things, it's not the result of their being particularly brave. Instead, they are responding to circumstances. I couldn't turn back. My cousin Paul looked at me and said, "Those dogs are going to bite you." When my parents asked him, "Well, Paul, aren't you going with him?" he was very clear that he was not. All that day he kept teasing me. I recognized, however, that he was only joking because he was very worried.

Later that day, my parents dropped me off at the church for the march.

What many people don't know about the Children's Crusade is how much preparation we received. First, the organizers met with us and asked us to watch a documentary about student protests in Nashville. Then they trained us to understand strategy and discipline and, quite frankly, the power of music. They knew the police officers were going to try to upset us and that when kids get upset, they can become very irrational and throw rocks or otherwise respond—and if you threw rocks at the police, they had a reason to put the dogs on you. So we were taught how to resist taunting from the police. Similarly, the organizers of the march knew that singing would elevate the experience, allowing us to block out the negativity and forget the fear we were experiencing. I was only twelve at the time but was in the ninth grade, having skipped two years of school, and I was mature for my age, so I was asked to lead a group of children—younger and older than me—within the march. As a group leader, I would help keep the group focused through singing and reminders to stay disciplined.

The Children's Crusade began on May 2. Almost a thousand students marched on City Hall that day, with more than six hundred arrested. The jails and detention centers were so full that Eugene "Bull" Connor, Birmingham's commissioner of public safety, attempted to dissuade further marching the next day, May 3, by using police dogs and fire cannons to turn back the children. Having seen this, I knew what we would be facing.

I marched on May 4. We left my church, Sixth Avenue Baptist, where I'd received training, went to Sixteenth Street Baptist, and then walked toward downtown. Though I do not have a great singing voice, I can carry a tune, and I had been taught to lead the other children in song. And so I sang one of the Negro spirituals:

> Ain't going to let nobody, turn me around
> Turn me around, turn me around
> Ain't going to let nobody turn me around
> Keep on a' walking. Keep on a' talking
> Marching up to freedom land

What is the most effective way to really upset children? Talking trash about their mothers. As expected, police officers lining the route taunted us and tried to get us to react. We had been trained to ignore their words and to focus on our goal of continuing downtown and kneeling on the steps of City Hall, and so we kept on marching and singing. The police then moved to contain the marchers, their dogs ready to attack. We could feel the tension when someone in the crowd threw a rock or when the dogs or fire hoses were brought near. And yet, because of the music and the discipline, the children continued moving in an orderly way. I was in a small group that broke off from the crowd as many other children were being stopped or detained.

I made it all the way to the steps of City Hall. What was my job when I got there? To kneel, to pray for our freedom, and to tell whoever was there our purpose: freedom to have the basic rights of other American citizens, to get a good education, and to have access to public accommodations, from water fountains and restrooms to restaurants and movie theaters. It was that simple. My students ask me, "Well, Doc, why would they put somebody in jail for that?" The law stated that you needed a permit to hold a protest, even a peaceful one, and the city withheld from Dr. King and the other leaders a permit to peacefully assemble.

I can't tell you how my knees were shaking as I arrived at the steps of City Hall. And who was there but Bull Connor himself. Connor, a former radio announcer, was in his sixth term as the elected official overseeing the city's police and fire departments. He was widely known for his aggressive support of the city's segregation ordinances. He had recently threatened to close and sell off the city's parks rather than follow a court order to integrate them. An imposing man with a booming voice, he was obviously angry on the day of the march because of the TV cameras. He looked at me and said, "What do you want, little Nigra?" Remember, I was not a courageous kid. I looked up at him, scared, and managed to say, in my Birmingham accent, "Suh, we want to kneel and pray." He spat in my face. Then my fellow demonstrators and I were gathered up and shoved into a police wagon waiting nearby.

Being in jail was an awful experience, and the guards made every effort to increase our misery. I was with a small group of boys from the march, and they put us in with the "bad boys"— juvenile delinquents who were in jail for real crimes. The guards encouraged these boys to be verbally and physically intimidating and abusive. We could hear kids hollering in other cells. Unspeakable things happened. I felt responsible to look out for the group of kids with me, even though they were not from my neighborhood and I did not know them. Only a couple of years younger than I, they would often cry that they wanted their mothers. I tried to keep them busy playing games. The only book in that place was the Bible—there were Bibles everywhere—so I would read to them. It turned out that one of the bad boys had been a student of my mother, so he gave us some protection. But when others would start coming toward my little group, I would read from scripture and have my kids quote after me, "The Lord is my shepherd. The Lord is my shepherd. I shall not want." Every time I read from the Bible, the bad boys would retreat: they didn't want to fight with God. I got that. It protected us.

In the middle of the week, when Dr. King and our parents gathered outside the detention center and held their vigil, we were reminded of our purpose in being there. We were all crying, but Dr. King assured us that our participation in the march, and our going to jail, would help make the world a better place for children not yet born. And though we may not have fully grasped the profound significance of that statement, his words gave us strength and invited us to think about the possibilities.

After five horrible days as encaged human beings, without the freedom to even breathe fresh air, we were released. I was excited to go back to school, Ullman High. I loved studying. I loved mathematics and reading. But my excitement turned to disappointment and anger when we discovered that the Board of Education had ordered the suspension of students who had been arrested for marching.

The way in which Ullman High School's principal, George Bell, handled our suspensions revealed the leader and role model that he was. In general, assemblies involving the whole school were very rare. However, Mr. Bell called the entire school together after he received word about the board's decision. It was clear that he did not want to suspend us, but as he had no choice, he decided to treat our suspensions like badges of courage. He used the ceremony reserved for inducting students into the National Honor Society to honor those of us who were now being suspended. A brilliant leader with a commanding voice, he called each of the children who had been in jail to the stage. He spoke to themes from Henry David Thoreau's work on civil disobedience to describe the importance of what we had accomplished. When he finished, the entire student body gave us a standing ovation. As we served our suspensions, Mr. Bell continued demonstrating what it means to be a leader. He and others worked around the bureaucracy, making sure we got notes from our classes and our homework assignments. He encouraged me to read Thoreau's "Civil Disobedience."

Initially, the local federal district court judge upheld the Board of Education action suspending us from school. We were in church that next week when we received the good news that the Fifth Circuit Court of Appeals—a court that handed down many decisions supporting civil rights—had reversed that ruling and that we could return to school. In fact, the Court of Appeals—composed of white southerners who nonetheless supported and advanced the civil rights of African Americans—went even further and condemned the board for its action. I will never forget both the tears of joy and spirit of celebration in that church that evening. We had been so afraid that we would not be able to continue our education.

In the meantime, the violent attacks by the city police and firemen on children engaged in peaceful protest had been captured in photographs and on film, and these images filled newspapers and television news for days, deeply affecting national sentiment, particularly in the North. Bull Connor had played the perfect foil, as civil rights leaders had hoped in picking Birmingham as a target in 1963. His tactics had backfired, and the tide soon turned. In June, an association representing most of the downtown stores negotiated an agreement with the SCLC leadership to desegregate within ninety days and to hire blacks in stores as salespeople and clerks.

That same month, on June 11, as the civil rights struggle continued in Alabama and across the South, President John F. Kennedy gave an impassioned and somewhat extemporaneous televised address to the nation advocating passage of civil rights legislation. In the address he said:

One hundred years of delay have passed since President Lincoln freed the slaves, yet their heirs, their grandsons, are not truly free. They are not yet freed from the bonds of injustice. They are not yet freed from social and economic oppression. And this nation, for all its hopes and all its boasts, will not be fully free until all its citizens are free.

We preach freedom around the world and we mean it. And we cherish our freedom here at home. But are we to say to the world—and much more importantly, to each other—that this is the land of the free, except for Negroes, that we have no second-class citizens, except Negroes, that we have no class or caste system, no ghettos, no master race, except with respect to Negroes?

Now, the time has come for this nation to fulfill its promise. The events in Birmingham and elsewhere have so increased the cries for equality that no city or state or legislative body can prudently choose to ignore them.

The fires of frustration and discord are burning in every city, North and South, where legal remedies are not at hand. Redress is sought in the streets, in demonstrations, parades, and protests which create tensions and threaten violence and threaten lives.

We face, therefore, a moral crisis as a country and a people. It cannot be met by repressive police action. It cannot be left to increased demonstrations in the streets. It cannot be quieted by token moves or talk. It is time to act in the Congress, in your state and local legislative bodies and, above all, in all of our daily lives.[24]

The experience of marching in the Children's Crusade in May 1963 taught me that even children can make decisions that have an impact on the rest of their lives, and that they know the difference between right and wrong. It also taught me that children can struggle to overcome challenges and be stronger as a result. When children have support, any struggle, whether it's standing up for civil rights or learning to read or solving math problems, can teach lessons about the importance of persistence. We all face struggles throughout our lives. What's important is how we respond. As children confront different problems and learn to handle them, they develop confidence. Success breeds success.

THE BOMBING OF THE SIXTEENTH STREET BAPTIST CHURCH

By September we were seeing signs of hope that desegregation was moving ahead in Birmingham—the agreement to desegregate downtown stores was being implemented, and the federal government brought pressure to integrate public elementary and secondary schools. To have the city leadership compromise with Dr. King and other civil rights leaders was a major victory. Things were finally changing.

But some in the Ku Klux Klan were not willing to let change happen peacefully. We were in church on Sunday, September 15, when our pastor was handed a note at the pulpit. He stopped preaching. This was the first time any of us could remember a church service being stopped midway through, so we began to imagine that this had to be bad. The preacher told us that Sixteenth Street Baptist Church—our sister church, attended by relatives, neighbors, and friends, and the center of the civil rights effort that year—had been bombed. My mother and father took us home, not knowing at the time whether other churches might also be targets for bombings.

I had friends at that church, including Cynthia Wesley, a classmate who had always treated me well. It was devastating to learn that Cynthia and three other girls had been killed. I had seen Cynthia just the Friday before, and I remember her saying as we left school that day, "Bye, Freeman. See you Monday." I'll never forget that moment—the kindness and hope in her eyes. Another of the girls had been given a ring that morning by her father. We heard that they had found her hand before they found her body. My friends and I had nightmares for years. It was as if we were in a war.[25]

My parents gave me permission to leave school to attend the funeral held for three of the girls at my church, Sixth Avenue Baptist, a few blocks away from my school.[26] Principal Bell, a mathematician and a hero of mine (especially after the march), saw me as I was preparing to leave, and said, "You are representing us today." Then he looked at my tie and thought that it was not dark enough for the occasion. He took off my tie, removed his own black tie, and tied it around my neck. Looking back on this, I am still amazed at the small things people can do to make a child feel special.

I will never forget the three caskets. Denise McNair was the youngest. I'd never seen a casket so small. Dr. King, despite facing criticism from some members of the community that the Children's Crusade and other activities he had helped organize were the cause of the bombing, returned to Birmingham and took responsibility. He looked into the faces of those parents. "At times," he said, "life is as hard, as hard as crucible steel."

LESSONS OF 1963

What gave me hope in the midst of the darkness that fell upon us with the church bombing was both experiencing the strong sense of community among blacks supporting each other and seeing many whites in my church for the first time. There were ministers, rabbis, and priests—people of God. It was amazing to see them all there, clearly expressing a sense of loss and grief. After those difficult times, my parents and many others worked to help us children get beyond the bitterness, the anger, even the hatred. Hate the action, not the person. Over and over, they said that hatred eats you on the inside.

This was the first lesson of the events of 1963 for me: it is important to place your life's experiences in perspective by understanding their context. From there you can better see the way forward. Years later, my mother called to tell me that Bull Connor, the Birmingham commissioner of public safety at the time of the Children's Crusade, had died. Connor had staunchly resisted all efforts to integrate Birmingham, and he was widely vilified for brutal tactics that resulted in civil rights protesters being attacked by police dogs and blasted with fire hoses. Yet I could tell my mother was crying as we spoke. I asked her why, saying, "This man was awful to us." Her response was powerful. She said, "Freeman, he was somebody's child." Her point was simply that he thought and acted as he did because of the way he was raised. That was an amazing moment of enlightenment for me. He was simply the product of his environment. One could respond that each of us can choose to rise above prejudices learned during childhood. Unfortunately, many do not.

I have often thought about that moment. It was my mother's way of giving me her faith in life itself and in humanity, but it was also her way of saying, "Put your own experiences in perspective." Part of being educated is being able to give context to whatever experiences you have had. Those who are able to do that can think more clearly about both the issues they face and ways to enable change in the world.

I really do believe Dr. King's words that we should strive for a world in which people are judged by the content of their character and not the color of their skin. Yet minorities and women have known for a long time that people tend, for example, to select people for educational opportunities and jobs who look like themselves.[27] Much of the time, this is not the result of any conscious animosity—people are simply most comfortable with what is familiar. A man selecting a new employee tends to focus on hiring another man in that position. Implicit biases, favorable and unfavorable, are developed over a lifetime, beginning in childhood, and when unexamined and unaddressed lead to disparities in health care, criminal justice, economic opportunity, and more.[28] Once our unconscious biases are recognized, however, they can be changed, because what we are dealing with as much as anything are expectations. I expect someone like me to act like me. I may have different expectations about someone who is "different," or I may have little experience upon which to formulate expectations in the first place. So providing people with positive expectations about people who are unlike themselves—demonstrating that others can perform well, too, and may bring different and valuable perspectives—can change their outlook and their actions.

One common human trait is a resistance to change. It often requires direct, personal experiences to overcome that resistance and serve as a catalyst. The media had a great impact on the civil rights movement by playing that role; television footage made a significant difference and helped transform the American psyche. While racial prejudice existed throughout the country, its daily reality was distant from many Americans. Television images broadcast in the 1960s allowed people in northern cities and elsewhere to see for the first time how harshly blacks were treated in the South and what was being done to children in defense of segregation.

The second lesson I learned was the importance of having high expectations and working hard. Growing up in Birmingham, I had the remarkable opportunity to interact with many people, in addition to my parents, who worked to instill these values as they helped me to be my very best. My high school counselor was Reverend John Wesley Rice Jr., Condoleezza Rice's father, who later became a university administrator, working as a dean at Stillman College and then assistant vice chancellor at the University of Denver. Reverend Rice was an inspiring educator who was particularly striking because of his keen intellect and dry wit. What made him so effective with students was his ability to encourage our curiosity, to answer questions with questions, to push us to think critically, and to empower us to see ourselves as serious thinkers. At the same time, he allowed us to laugh and be children.

When we were suspended from school after the march, Reverend Rice and our teachers were concerned, of course, about our academic progress, and they wanted to make sure we were okay. What Reverend Rice did, both as my counselor and during youth discussion groups he held in the community, was to give us opportunities to reflect on our experiences, to learn more about leadership, and to understand the stories of those people of color who had striven for excellence and succeeded. He was always listening to the voices of children and pushing us to think more critically than we might have imagined. He was also the first person to teach me that it was possible to make a joke or deliver a funny comment without so much as a smile. He was so smart that his comments often went over our heads, causing us to laugh only later when we realized what he meant. Condoleezza Rice and I had very similar backgrounds. We both were very fortunate to have been raised by hardworking Christian parents who made us their top priority.

Many of the people I grew up with have gone on to amazing success. Ms. Rice, a scholar specializing in Soviet and Russian affairs, became a professor at Stanford and then the university's provost. She later served as national security advisor and then secretary of state. Mary

Bush is one of the most successful women in corporate America, having served in high-level financial positions in the US Treasury Department, in senior-level positions in finance in New York, and as the US government's representative on the International Monetary Fund Board. Angela Davis became a civil rights leader and was one of the most famous black women activists in the 1960s. She was a faculty member at the University of California, Los Angeles, and later at the University of California, Santa Cruz, and at Syracuse University. Tommy Wright, a mathematician, heads the Statistical Research Division at the US Bureau of the Census. Joe Gale became a chemist and then president of Talladega College. Alma Vivian Powell, wife of Colin Powell, is chair of America's Promise Alliance, a national organization that promotes youth development and education. Alma's father had been principal of Alabama's largest high school for blacks, Parker High School. More important for me, her uncle was my beloved high school principal, Mr. Bell, who would come into our class, place a math problem on the board, and challenge us to solve it later, with the reward of a dime. I was determined to get that dime every time—both because it symbolized being the best and because with it I could buy ten Tootsie Rolls. Large numbers of other young people from my community went on to earn graduate degrees and are now educators, physicians, judges, lawyers, entrepreneurs, and professionals throughout America.

These were all family friends. They and their parents inspired me and affirmed what my parents constantly preached—that nothing takes the place of hard work. In the words of Aristotle, "Excellence is never an accident."

The message that so many black children in the Deep South heard was: "The world is not fair. What do you do about it? Don't expect fairness, just work to be twice as good." The emphasis in my community, from teachers and principals like Mr. Bell, was on high achievement, on working to be your very best. You weren't expecting anyone to give you anything.[29]

Years later, as I worked with colleagues to study lessons learned from our experience with a program designed to support high-achieving minorities in the STEM disciplines, I was not surprised to discover that many of these high-achieving students of all races had been exposed to the same practices and values that have sustained so many Americans and that characterized my own experience in Birmingham. Their parents emphasized good communication, recognized the importance of reading skills, and set high expectations. It was reaffirming to see that, with all the changes in our society, some fundamental principles remain important.

My colleagues and I use that same philosophy with our students today. We want them to dream about the possibilities and to appreciate the strong connection between hard work and success. When students enter our university, UMBC—even high-achieving high school graduates—few understand how hard they will need to work to excel. Achieving excellence in STEM disciplines is especially challenging because students must constantly keep up with the work. If a student misses class or fails to study for a few days, it is usually difficult to catch up. And just like my childhood friends, many students do not necessarily know just how high their goals can be set or what the possibilities are for the future. Most important, students are most likely to excel when they, their parents, and their teachers set high and clear expectations. As the late Benjamin Mays, president of Morehouse College, said, "It must be borne in mind that the tragedy of life doesn't lie in not reaching your goal. The tragedy lies in having no goal to reach. It isn't a calamity to die with dreams unfulfilled, but it is a calamity not to dream. It is not a disaster to be unable to capture your ideal, but it is a disaster to have no ideal to capture. It is not a disgrace not to reach the stars, but it is a disgrace to have no stars to reach for. Not failure, but low aim is sin."[30]

2

Development of an Educator

Progress toward the desegregation of schools in the South ordered in *Brown v. Board of Education* was uneven at best, despite a second ruling in 1955 that set out actions for implementing its original decision. In Baltimore, there had already been a small step toward integration before *Brown*, when fifteen black students were admitted to an advanced program in engineering at Baltimore Polytechnic Institute, a city high school, in 1952, because there was no comparable, segregated program for blacks. Encouraged by this, the president of the Baltimore City school board, Walter Sondheim, pushed for full desegregation of city schools in 1954.[1] But farther south, there was substantial resistance. In 1957, for example, when Little Rock public school officials moved forward with a plan to integrate the city's high schools, segregationist groups opposed the plan, and Governor Orval Faubus supported

55

them by sending Arkansas National Guard troops to keep black students from enrolling at Central High School, whose student body was all-white. President Eisenhower took control away from Faubus by federalizing the Arkansas National Guard and then sent in federal troops from the 101st Airborne to protect nine black students who then enrolled in and attended Central.

In 1963, almost a decade after the *Brown* decision and despite integration efforts in other states, Alabama still maintained segregated schools, and integration would only arrive with further struggle. On June 11, Alabama governor George Wallace, who had vowed "segregation now, segregation tomorrow, segregation forever!" in his inaugural address, famously took his "stand in the schoolhouse door" at the University of Alabama to bar the registration of black students. In so doing, he forced a showdown with President Kennedy, who then federalized the Alabama National Guard and commanded its general to order Wallace to move aside. After a speech that argued for states' rights, Wallace reluctantly did so. Under the protection of the National Guard, students Vivian Malone and James Hood later quietly registered. This showdown was the final chapter in a story that had actually begun in 1952, when Autherine Lucy and Polly Anne Myers had attempted to enroll at Alabama for graduate school. Their initial applications had been accepted but then denied once the university discovered the race of the two women. This led to a lawsuit that was decided post-*Brown* in favor of Lucy and Myers in 1955. Lucy was admitted and began attending classes in February 1956. However, after she was attacked by a mob of white students, Lucy was removed from campus "for her own protection." Now, in 1963, Malone and Hood were able to attend, and Malone earned her bachelor's degree in business management.[2]

On July 12, 1963, the US Fifth Circuit Court of Appeals finally ruled in a case filed years earlier that the integration of Birmingham's public schools must begin immediately, but again the process would be strongly, even violently, opposed and would again eventually require federal intervention. The Birmingham Public Schools developed a plan to begin integration with Graymont Elementary School, West End High School, and Ramsay High School in September. James Armstrong, a barber who also served as security chief for the Alabama Christian Movement for Human Rights, was the parent who had filed the successful lawsuit. On September 4, he arrived at Graymont Elementary with his sons Dwight and Floyd, and accompanied by Fred Shuttlesworth and their attorney, Oscar Adams, to enroll the boys for the school year, as he was legally entitled to do. The Armstrongs were met at the front door by a crowd of white students and parents opposed to integration. Ultimately, they found their way into the school by another door, picked up the enrollment forms they needed, and quickly and quietly left.[3] That night a bomb was detonated at the home of a civil rights activist, and the school superintendent, citing the prospect of violence the next day, temporarily closed city schools. Upon the schools' reopening five days later, on September 9, Governor Wallace sent state police to encircle them and keep them closed. This again forced President Kennedy to federalize the Alabama National Guard and send it to ensure that the schools opened the following day. On September 10, the Armstrongs attended Graymont, and the first black students were also escorted by the National Guard into Ramsay and West End High Schools. The next day, September 11, a white teenager threw a rock through the windshield of the car taking Patricia Marcus and Josephine Powell, two black students, home from West End. But the worst was yet to come. On September 15, as I recounted in chapter 1, Klansmen enraged by desegregation bombed the Sixteenth Street Baptist Church, a tragedy that took the lives of four little girls.

With the possibility of desegregation and also the probability of violence, my parents and I struggled to assess what might be gained or lost were I one of the children to integrate all-white Ramsay High School in September. The benefits of attending a better-resourced school were certainly obvious and appealing. On the other hand, my parents worried about exposing me to the violence of those who opposed integration. They remembered the violence that Reverend Shuttlesworth and his wife had experienced when they had tried to enroll their children at Phillips High School in 1957, as well as what had happened to countless others who sought to integrate schools across the South since 1954. And my mother, a teacher, had a deeper concern. Yes, the resources of the white schools were superior. But black children would be attending a school in which they were not wanted, not just by the other students but also by many of the teachers and administrators. She understood that the attitude of a teacher can mean everything in shaping the sense of self—the sense of autonomy and possibility—for a child.[4]

So, their compromise, because I wanted to see what

education was like in the larger world, was to send me "to the North" for a summer. We had been invited to participate in a movement spearheaded by the Society of Friends (Quakers) to bring black children north to live in the homes of Quakers in Pennsylvania and elsewhere.[5] For example, the Davis girls from Birmingham, Angela Davis and her sister, whose mother was one of my teachers, went. This opportunity was enticing, but to feel comfortable sending me north, my parents wanted me to live with someone they knew. I had a godmother who once taught with my mother in Birmingham and now taught in Springfield, Massachusetts—a state we considered a place of high culture, with an emphasis on education, universities, and arts institutions. The solution for my parents, then, was to send me to live with my godmother for a summer in Springfield, where I would take high school classes and have access to a number of cultural opportunities, including visiting the museums of Boston.

SPRINGFIELD, MASSACHUSETTS (SUMMER 1964)

The summer before I entered eleventh grade, my cousin Paul and I attended Springfield's technical high school, where I studied pre-calculus and chemistry. I was thirteen years old and this was the first time that I attended school with white children. It was clear to me from the first day of school in Springfield that the education offered there was far more advanced and rigorous than what black children were receiving in Birmingham. (It was only later that I learned that education in the North was also far superior to what many white kids in the South were receiving as well.) The other students were older, generally sixteen and seventeen, but while I had to work harder than ever, I found that I could keep up, and I enjoyed the rigor.

I had one major problem in Springfield: nobody in the all-white school I attended would speak to me. Every now and then one girl would respond to my "Good morning" with "Hi," but as a rule nobody talked to me. I seemed invisible even to the teachers. When a teacher asked a question, even if mine was the only hand in the air, he or she would look straight through me. Not once did a teacher speak to me; it was an awful experience. I appreciated Ralph Ellison's *Invisible Man* after that. The irony, of course, is that it was precisely the racist attitudes held by teachers in the white schools in Birmingham that I had come to Massachusetts to avoid. A child never forgets how a teacher treats him or her. You never forget feeling that you are not valued. But when I called home and told my parents about my experiences and how badly I felt, what did they tell me? "You know how much we love you and how special you are, but you are not there to be liked. You're there to get the education." They felt badly, but they were trying to toughen me for life's realities. Again, there was no time to be a victim; I was to take advantage of what was given to me.

Despite the unfortunate social environment in the Massachusetts school, I understood just how strong the education was there when I returned to all-black Ullman High in the accelerated section of the eleventh grade. My classmates at Ullman were also older than me, and many had been A students during the first two years of high school. However, because of the instruction I received in Springfield, I had already studied the material that would be covered in my eleventh-grade year, a situation that allowed me to excel but also brought some frustration. My Springfield studies prepared me to earn the highest scores in mathematics and science throughout the year— my score might be in the upper 90s and the next-highest score in the low 80s. But the teacher would give all of the top scores As. I thought that was unfair at first, but my parents helped me to understand that it was not that I was smarter than the other kids but, rather, that I had had the advantage of stronger preparation.

My mother's suggestion to me was to work with those students who had not had the same academic experiences as I to help them develop a stronger grasp of the material. I did, and it opened my eyes to the challenge of understanding how children learn. My teacher had encouraged me to tutor one or two other students in reading from the time I was in first grade (which I attended from age four to age six), and this, I learned, helped me as much as those I helped. But tutoring other students in mathematics in high school, I found that it was much more challenging to explain concepts with clarity and to work with students as they struggled with word problems than it was for me to simply take a test and perform. I then began to observe how my teachers approached the work. They were not just caring, they understood the wide range of backgrounds that students brought to class, and they adjusted their approaches as they worked with individual children. The lesson I learned was that we should have high expectations for each student, assessing what his or her skills and knowledge are, and build from there. I also learned that peer-to-peer tutoring can play an invaluable role in teaching and learning.

TUSKEGEE INSTITUTE (SUMMER 1965)

Following eleventh grade, I participated in a summer program in mathematics and statistics for high-achieving black students, sponsored by the National Science Foundation and held at the Tuskegee Institute (now Tuskegee University), a historically black college like Alabama State and Hampton. Participants came from all over the country, so this was the second summer in a row that I spent with kids from the North, this time black. I now discovered that many of these students from the North who attended integrated public or private schools were also better prepared than I was. I was better in mathematics than most southern kids because of my Springfield experience, but I was both fascinated and inspired by just how much better prepared these kids from the North were, not only in mathematics but other subjects as well. They were much more accustomed to years of rigorous problem-solving. Their ability to analyze was stronger. Their explanations were clearer.

It was here that I first experienced the power of community and the power of working in groups. On the first day of class, the mathematics professor wrote out a problem on the board and asked us, "Who can solve it?" He was purposefully challenging us, because we thought we were so smart, but he had a further message as well. Initially nobody could solve the problem, so he said, "When you can solve it, come see me." Everybody got upset, thinking, "He's the teacher. If we can't do it, he's supposed to show us how." But after we'd struggled individually for some time, he encouraged us to work together, identifying the questions about the problem that we were having the toughest time with. These were beyond our grasp individually, but—after much frustration—we found we were able to solve the problem when we worked together. There was a growing synergy in the group as we admitted what we did not understand and shared information with one another. By the end of the summer, many of us had come to appreciate the value of collaboration. When you have a community of students who trust one another, they can push one another to excel. If you can create the right culture, the kids at the bottom can improve with the help not only of teachers but of other students.

It was also during my summer at the Tuskegee Institute that I formed a sense of myself academically and professionally. During that first class, I said, referring to the teacher, "Who is that guy?" and the other students said, "Dr. So-and-so." I said, "Doctor? He's not a physician; he's a teacher." They said, "No, not an MD. He's a PhD." I said, "What's a PhD?" They said, "That's the highest degree you can get," and I said, "That's what I'm going to get." At age fourteen, I started looking in the mirror every morning saying, "Good morning, Dr. Hrabowski." I wanted to be this person who was really exciting people about mathematics. And one day later in college, Jackie Coleman, my girlfriend, saw me talking to my reflection and remarked, "You know, you really are crazy." But this is, again, the point about the influence of teachers—the flip side of the negative impact of the white teachers in Springfield. If a teacher helps a child to develop a strong sense of self, to imagine what he or she wants to be, all things are possible.

HAMPTON INSTITUTE (1966-70)

When it was time for me to go to college, my parents
again had to weigh the advantages and disadvantages
of integrated schools. I had been recruited by predominantly white institutions in New England, but my parents remembered how concerned they had been and how
unhappy I had felt after my experience in Springfield,
even though I had learned a great deal. As graduates of
historically black colleges, my parents truly believed that
these institutions would provide a more nurturing environment for me. I had been invited to attend Morehouse
College in Atlanta on early admission at the end of my
eleventh-grade year. However, my mother thought that at
age fourteen I was just too young. By the next year, they
reaffirmed their wish for me to attend Morehouse because
of its reputation for preparing young black men, the most
famous being Dr. King, and because its president, Dr. Benjamin Mays, was one of the most admired black college
presidents since Booker T. Washington. However, since
I had been so disappointed that they had prevented me
from attending the prior year, I rebelled and went all the
way "north to Virginia" to attend the Hampton Institute
(now Hampton University). I had been very impressed by
Tuskegee, and so I went to Hampton, the alma mater of
Booker T. Washington, Tuskegee's founder.

I began my Hampton experience in 1966. During that
summer after high school, I participated in Project SPUR,
a program created for high-achieving entering Hampton freshmen. Here again, I was immediately reminded
that academic preparation in the North was stronger, as
Hampton had different admissions standards for students
from the South and North. The students participating in

the summer program from the South were required to be at the very top of their classes—valedictorian or salutatorian. If they were from the North, however, they were required only to be in the top 10 percent of their class. At first, those of us from the South found this unfair and were unhappy with the geographically based admissions standards. However, we came to understand that this stemmed from the fact that kids from some parts of the country were, overall, better prepared.

My perspective on my own preparation and skill level changed on the day we received the scores from our first test in calculus class. The professor said she would call the grades in order. I assumed that I, as always, would have the highest grade. But my name was not called first this time. Or second. When she got to the ninth name, still not mine, tears were running down my face. I finally understood that I was not the smartest black kid in the world. Only one person got 100, a cute girl named Jackie Coleman. I was such an immature fifteen-year-old that I hollered out, "I'm going to marry her one day." And in fact, I did, right after we graduated in 1970.

The lesson of Hampton Institute—that academic preparation was uneven racially and geographically—was reinforced the next summer, after my freshman year, when I took Calculus III at the University of Alabama at Birmingham. After I had received the highest test scores in that class, the professor, a white man, asked me, "Where did you go to school?"—by which he meant, "How can a black student get the top grade in this class?" To be fair, he wasn't being rude or condescending; he had simply not expected it. I had had a stronger education than many blacks, and that was reinforced by my

Springfield experience and the rigorous work I had done in pre-calculus. But this further enlightened me about academic preparation, demonstrating that black children were not the only ones who were not getting a good education in the South—many white children were not well prepared either. I understood that educational quality in the United States had both regional and racial dimensions, leading to academic-achievement gaps that linger today. (Later, at the University of Illinois, I would learn about the further urban-suburban dimension that was correlated, at the time, with both race and socioeconomic status.)

This important lesson led me to think about strategies for addressing these inequalities, and my years as an undergraduate taught me two additional valuable lessons that would shape my path through graduate school and my career in administration. The first was the power of community: it supported us as we struggled with the work, it helped overcome differences in academic preparation, and it allowed us to persist when we might otherwise have given up. A central aspect of the Hampton experience was that I tutored many students, worked regularly with better-prepared students, and had meaningful relationships with professors. I also learned the importance of explaining concepts and that it was much more difficult for me to help a fellow student get an A or B than for me to get an A or B myself. Understanding something intuitively does not necessarily mean that you can explain the concept with clarity to every person, because people learn in different ways.

The second realization I had in my undergraduate years had to do with the power of identity; specifically, the influence of one's self-perception and identification with a possible career on whether you went toward or away from STEM disciplines. My classmate (and later wife) Jackie Coleman was extraordinarily talented in math. She had been the Virginia Champion (a math competition among black high schools) in geometry two years before our freshman year at Hampton, and she always earned As in math, a subject she loved. I was fascinated by her ability to connect geometry to her experiences with her father, a home builder and science teacher. Her excitement about lines, angles, and degrees, and her perceptions about structures, mixtures, proportions, ratios, and relationships were clearly the result of hands-on experience in applying mathematics to real life—to, for example, three-dimensional structures. In calculus, she could actually see the structures as we learned to compute the area of different figures using the integral function. Nevertheless, she refused to consider majoring in math because she couldn't see a career in which she could use it. She did not want to teach (she was shy), and she'd never heard of a woman architect. So she chose to major in psychology because of her interest in human behavior, completing a math minor for the fun of it, and she excelled in graduate statistics courses in educational psychology and early-child development. She went on from there to a very successful career with T. Rowe Price, yet one wonders what else she might have done if just one teacher had encouraged her in mathematics. No teacher had ever told her that her aptitude in math was such that she should consider majoring and pursuing a career in it.

Another experience of the power of an individual's self-perception related to my college roommate of three years at Hampton, Ronnie Belton. He took great pride in being a stellar track athlete (including eventually being captain of the track team), but he was consistently self-effacing about his academic work and especially didn't like math. However, he was one of the smartest, clearest-thinking people I'd ever met. He always asked penetrating questions, including about mathematics. He completed a major in sociology and worked for the Urban League. Ronnie later went on to become one of the first black stockbrokers in Florida, and now serves as the chief financial officer for the city of Jacksonville. This is a great success, yet it raises the question of whether he would have pursued mathematics or science at a younger age had he been a member of a learning community that affirmed identification with one of these disciplines.

UNIVERSITY OF ILLINOIS (1970–75)

In the fall of 1970 I entered the University of Illinois at Champaign-Urbana, a school I had chosen because one of my professors at Hampton, Dr. Geraldine Darden, had earned her PhD in mathematics there. I had known for some time that I would go to graduate school in mathematics, and I was excited to be at Illinois. However, the experiences I had there as, typically, the only black student in my mathematics classes, and my observations about the preparation of black students from Chicago with whom I worked, would transform my career goals, research, and educational philosophy and set me on a different path for the next four decades.

When I started graduate school, I found that while I was academically prepared for the work in mathematics,

I was not prepared for the isolation I would feel. I had not felt this alone since the summer I spent in Springfield while in high school. I was usually the only African American student in my classes, and it was clear that people were unaccustomed to having someone who looked like me in class and, in some cases, did not expect me to do well. One mathematics professor even wrote on my exam after I earned an A minus that I had done "surprisingly well." It was clear to me that most of the mathematics professors at Illinois at that time had had few if any blacks in their graduate classes and had never seen blacks succeed, and because of this they were "surprised" when they encountered a black student who excelled. In 1941 David Blackwell became the first African American to earn a PhD in the mathematics department at Illinois. My professor later conceded that I had taught him more about life than he had taught me about math. My success had opened his eyes.

Some of the discouraging experiences I had in graduate school had nothing to do with race. For example, one day that same semester, another of my mathematics professors wrote a proof on the board, moving directly from step one to step five with no explanation of steps two, three, and four. I did not see how he arrived at step five. I had been accustomed, as an undergraduate at a liberal arts college, to ask questions in class, so I asked, "I can get to steps two and three, even four, but how did you get to step five?" He looked at me and said with a smirk, "Isn't it obvious?" Everyone in the class smirked as well. I thought, "If it were obvious, I wouldn't have asked you the question." I never asked another question in that class. But that was not the end of the matter. My professors at Hampton had told me, "Don't let anyone intimidate you so much that you don't go and ask questions. Even when they seem like they are tired of you, just smile, be humble, and say, 'But I need your help.'" I went to that professor who had been so condescending to me in class and politely bugged him, returning again and again, determined to learn everything I could from him. When the midterm papers were later handed back to us, I looked around and saw several Cs—a flunking grade in graduate school—while I had earned an A minus. I held my paper up and said, "I guess it was kind of obvious." Most of the class, it turned out, had been as confused by the proof as I had been.

I realized that many minority students had much more fundamental problems, including insufficient preparation, lack of role models, and insufficiently high expectations for them from faculty. While at Illinois, I worked in one of the residence halls, where I came into contact with many undergraduates, including black students. Illinois had admitted its first large group of black undergraduates in 1968, and many of these students, and those who came after them, would engage me in conversation about their problems. Kids from Chicago, in particular, who had been the best in mathematics and science in their high schools but were not performing well in college would ask, "Do you think I'm dumb? Why is it that the white kids are getting As and I can't even pass?" I would tell them that the difference was not due to any lack of intelligence but to the differences between the academic preparation that students received in most inner-city schools compared to that provided in suburban schools. The white students had stronger backgrounds because their schools had been more rigorous and the education more advanced.

In addition to insufficient preparation, these undergraduates had almost no African American role models once they arrived at college. There were some exceptions, to be sure. Several black administrators and advanced graduate students served as role models for many of us. Two of the most admired were Dean Clarence Shelley in Student Affairs, my first full-time boss, and Jim Anderson, now a prominent professor and academic administrator at Illinois. These men showed us that African American males could succeed in a predominantly white environment. The black couple who had the most influence on Jackie and me was Richard and Mildred Barksdale. Richard had come to Illinois as a tenured faculty member in literature and associate dean of the graduate school. Mildred served as assistant dean in the College of Liberal Arts and Sciences. They were impressive, and a source of advice and inspiration for us. Greta Hogan, a white woman from New York, also served as a mentor for me. Greta was an administrator in student services who worked with me on a college preparatory program for disadvantaged high school students that I staffed. Greta, whose husband was on the faculty, was strongly committed to helping low-income children and youth. She taught me how to write about complex topics in clear, simple prose; she helped me appreciate the power of language to influence the thinking of others; and, like my mother, she challenged me to read more broadly. She was the harshest critic of my writing and the person who inspired me to take courses in literary criticism and British literature.

Beyond the Barksdales, though, the mentors who could serve as role models for African American students at Illinois were few. There were only three other African American students in the mathematics graduate program, and we knew of no African American professors in mathematics or other STEM disciplines at the university. There was one—and only one—female mathematics professor at Illinois, and she was not on the tenure track. When I was in one of her classes, she gave me a look, and the look said, "I understand." For the first time, I comprehended that there were these parallel worlds that women and people of color inhabited. Just like blacks, women often found themselves in situations in which they were the only one, and in those situations many of them assumed that they could not succeed—as mathematics professors, for example. She was very helpful in discussing the academic work and encouraging me. I did, of course, realize that some white, male faculty could be helpful as well. One of them was thoughtful enough to go over difficult algebraic proofs with me and to remark, "You are very unusual." While this did reflect the general "bigotry of low expectations" I noted above, it was heartening that he could rise above them and it taught me that others could, too, when they worked with an African American who could excel.

After seeing the problems that many minority students were having, I felt an important need for more structure to support them. I established an informal mathematics tutorial center in one of the residence halls, a center that would support black undergraduate and graduate students in the social sciences and business who were having problems with statistics and other quantitative courses. For four years, I also directed the Upward Bound program for high school students in the tenth through twelfth grades. This program, first authorized by the Higher Education Act of 1965, provided college-prep classes during the summer and follow-up activities, including tutoring, during the school year. The students participating in our program were mainly first-generation Americans, minorities, or both, and many of them were the sons and daughters of black people who worked in the homes of the University of Illinois faculty and staff. We operated the program after school, year-round, several days during the week and on Saturdays. We focused on preparation for college and careers, providing tutoring and advising, instruction in reading and mathematics, and a variety of cultural activities such as visiting museums and attending plays.

I spent many hours talking with Upward Bound staff about issues involving minority-student achievement, as we were constantly wrestling with questions about students' academic performance. My experience with these students and others needing developmental work in mathematics and reading helped me to understand what sometimes happens to students whose academic preparation is significantly below the level required for success. We find that an environment challenging in terms of both academics and race can shake students' confidence and leave them feeling incapable or less able—and often less motivated—to overcome obstacles and succeed. This is especially true for students in STEM—disciplines in which one course builds on another and where falling behind in one course often means underperforming in subsequent courses, just as in foreign language training. It rarely happens that a student with a weak pre-calculus background performs successfully in a career in engineering.

As I moved through my master's program, I continued to enjoy mathematics, yet my sense of isolation and my awareness of an important issue to be addressed—the needs of minority students in STEM—made it difficult for me to imagine spending another four or five years by myself in the doctoral program in mathematics. So I changed course. I was impressed by the chancellor of the University of Illinois, John Corbally, who had a PhD in educational administration and finance, as well as by David Dodds Henry, a former president of the University of Illinois who was on the faculty in higher education administration when I was there. I had also become fascinated by the work of the Educational Testing Service, because I wanted to learn much more about why black children were not performing well on standardized tests. As I worked with Upward Bound students to prepare them for the Scholastic Aptitude Test (SAT), I saw an important connection between reading well and being able to solve word problems, both in general and more specifically on standardized tests. So I left the mathematics program after completing my master's degree. My interest and preparation in mathematics proved quite helpful in convincing the admissions committee of the university's doctoral program in higher education administration to allow me to enter that program, with a focus on statistics and evaluation, through the Department of Educational Psychology. This shift led to my teaching a graduate statistics course in educational psychology and helping students in their graduate statistics courses and with their doctoral dissertations. Most important, I de-

cided to focus my research on minority-student performance in mathematics, science, and engineering. For the
past forty years, I have spent much of my professional career addressing that issue and helping minority students
excel in these areas. In fact, my first article focused on
this topic, "Graduate School Success of Black Students
from Black and White Colleges," in which my coauthor
and I argued that graduate students in science were more
likely to be graduates of historically black colleges and
university (HBCUs) than of predominantly white institutions. We found that there was no difference in performance between blacks from the two types of institutions,
but blacks who had gone to the smaller HBCUs tended
to have more self-confidence and a stronger sense of self.[6]

ACADEMIC ADMINISTRATION

My time working as a young academic administrator also
shaped my professional goals. While at the University
of Illinois, in addition to working in the residence halls
I worked as an assistant dean in student services and an
administrative intern in the College of Liberal Arts and
Sciences. In all of these roles, I learned a great deal about
the need to address the "whole student," including students' motivation, academic preparation, residential life,
social integration, family issues, and financial aid. All of
these were linked and all had to be supported. All my life
I had learned from my parents about the challenges of engaging students—including moments of excitement when
children were excelling and moments of frustration when
students were not. The problem of engagement was multi-
faceted, involving many aspects of the life of the student.

For example, I was always fascinated when my father sent one of his fellow workers from the steel mill to my mother for a GED class. The discussion between my parents focused on the ways to encourage the student and the challenges that some of the guys—even those who were quite smart—faced in balancing work, family, and study. Their attitude was that it just takes time and practice to acquire the skills.

Afterwards, I briefly served as associate dean of the graduate school at Alabama A&M and taught freshman mathematics and graduate courses in statistics there. But my real focus at this time was the academic preparation of students, including testing, placement, and academic performance. While at A&M, I gave several conference presentations—for the federal TRIO Programs and the National Association for Equal Opportunity in Higher Education (NAFEO), among others—on remediation and the need to strengthen reading and mathematics instruction for students who were poorly prepared. These talks brought me to the attention of Coppin State College (now Coppin State University) in Baltimore City, which invited me to interview for the position of dean of arts and sciences, a position I was offered in 1977 and then held for six years before becoming vice president for academic affairs in 1983 (thus fulfilling my dream since Tuskegee of becoming a PhD, a professor, and a dean).

At Coppin, I focused on further understanding the academic preparation of students and the relationship between that and their performance in first-year courses. I learned, or had reinforced, four key lessons. First, many students at Coppin, particularly those from Baltimore City, were underprepared and needed more instructional time, and yet were very bright. These students could achieve academic success when motivated to do so. Second, as was true for me at Tuskegee and in other situations, students' having a small group of peers as a network for solving mathematics problems and discussing personal issues was an essential part of success at every level. I encouraged students to work together, to focus on the work, and to become an effective problem-solving team. When students work together and accept help, learning can improve substantially. Third, attitude is everything. If a student is willing to take advice, attend class, participate in supplemental work, admit when she or he does not understand, accept help, and persist, that student is likely to succeed. Without a doubt, for example, adult students returning to college after working for some time, especially adult women, tended to be more successful. They understood the relationship between getting an education and a degree and their future success. Their families' futures, their children, depended on their incomes, and so they were motivated. Fourth, if a professor has a strong motivation to teach students with academic challenges, the student is more likely to succeed. Further, if the faculty member's past experience working with students needing remediation has been successful, building their academic skills, the probability of success for current students increases even more.

A CAREER FOCUSED ON STUDENT SUCCESS

For the past forty years, I have focused on increasing the participation and success of students in mathematics, science, and engineering. Even before then, as a student in elementary and high school, I noticed that when the teacher turned her back on the math class, most of the kids started doing other things. It was puzzling to me; I loved math so much it gave me goose bumps. Yet, others were not excited about math at all. My first question, then, was, "How can we excite children about math and science?" When I was in graduate school, I saw how isolated minority students could feel and what a difference additional support—academic and social—could make. So my second question was, "What strategies can we develop to help minority students, women, and students in general do well in mathematics and science and increase their presence in the faculty?" Most broadly, my third question was, "How can we have an America in which people of color and women are fully expected to do as well as anyone else in their disciplines? How do we change the mindset of teachers, professors, and employers so that many more students succeed?"

To answer these questions, I drew on the many experiences I had had from my childhood in Birmingham, Springfield, and Tuskegee, to those when I was older in Hampton, Illinois, and Coppin. I drew on what I learned about how sufficient preparation, high expectations, and the attitudes of students, teachers, and administrators shaped a student's dreams and success. I reflected on the importance of addressing the whole student, bringing students together as part of a community, and providing role models who help guide students in their studies and careers. I understood that successful programs must help students identify what they do not know, ask for help, work in groups, and embrace hard work.

3

Inclusive Excellence
in Science and Engineering

In early 1987 I was recruited to work at UMBC as vice provost by Michael Hooker, the university's president. Having already served as vice president for academic affairs at Coppin, I felt well prepared to focus on the academic performance of undergraduates in this newly created position. Taking this position would lead, the next year, to perhaps the most important encounter of my career, when I met Baltimore philanthropist Robert Meyerhoff, who was seriously concerned about the lack of opportunities for young black men and wanted to use his resources to provide support. This moment gave me the chance to propose an approach to attacking the problem of underrepresentation of African American students in STEM fields at UMBC that could be replicated by other institutions. Thus began the Meyerhoff Scholars Program, which has become one of the most important programs for educating African Americans committed to earning PhDs in the natural sciences and engineering.

My experience and the lessons I had learned over the years served me well when the opportunity came to develop this program—an important experiment the success of which was far from certain. As with many other predominantly white institutions, UMBC had made some progress in improving the academic success of African American students in the humanities and social sciences, but we had made only very little progress in the natural sciences and engineering. In fact, when I searched for a predominantly white institution that had been successful in developing and implementing a program that led to even five students excelling in STEM and going on to complete doctorates, I could not find any. The late Michael Hooker, UMBC president at the time, provided the leadership, encouragement, and support for my colleagues and me to undertake this uncertain experiment. Now, more than two decades later, we have demonstrated what works. We have produced a model program that other universities are seeking to emulate.

NATIONAL CONTEXT

In 2005 Senators Lamar Alexander (R-TN) and Jeff Bingaman (D-NM) asked the National Academy of Sciences to produce a report that would provide the top ten actions Congress could take to ensure the United States remained a global leader in science and engineering and used that leadership to power our economy. The National Academies, through a committee chaired by Norman Augustine (former chair and CEO of Lockheed Martin), quickly produced a powerful narrative about the importance of innovation to global economic competitiveness in the twenty-first century, and the central role played by science and engineering education and research in innovation. The committee's report, *Rising Above the Gathering Storm*, provided recommendations for K–12 science and mathematics education; higher education in science, mathematics, and engineering; federal funding for research; and ways to enable innovation in the economy.[1] The report focused on ensuring a robust pipeline of students in science and engineering, with an emphasis on preparing more qualified K–12 teachers in science and mathematics.

The report had a powerful impact, leading directly to passage by Congress of the America COMPETES Act of 2007.[2] But the report was deficient in one important way: it did not address the relationship between competitiveness and the nation's changing demographics. The racial and ethnic groups most underrepresented in science and engineering were the fastest growing in the US population, projected to comprise nearly half that population by 2050. In addition to addressing issues of fairness and equity, the United States needed to develop a strategy for actively increasing diversity in science and engineering in order to ensure that we had a robust twenty-first-century science and engineering workforce.

Even as Congress considered the America COMPETES Act, Senators Edward Kennedy (D-MA), Hillary Clinton (D-NY), Barbara Mikulski (D-MD), and Patty Murray (D-WA) asked the National Academies to undertake a follow-up study focused on increasing the participation and success of underrepresented minorities in the natural sciences and engineering. The National Academies responded by appointing a committee that I had the privilege to chair, and in 2011 we produced a new report, *Expanding Underrepresented Minority Participation: America's Science and Technology Talent at the Crossroads*.[3] The committee set out the dimensions of the problem as follows:

> The S&E [science and engineering] workforce is large and fast-growing: more than 5 million strong and pro-jected by the US Bureau of Labor Statistics to grow faster than any other sector in the coming years. This growth rate provides an opportunity as well as an obligation to *draw on new sources of talent to make the S&E workforce as robust and dynamic as possible* [emphasis added]. But we start from a challenging position: Underrepresented minority groups comprised 28.5 percent of our national population in 2006, yet just 9.1 percent of college-educated Americans in science and engineering occu-pations (academic and nonacademic), suggesting the proportion of underrepresented minorities would need to *triple* to match their share of the overall US popula-tion. Underrepresentation of this magnitude in the S&E workforce stems from the underproduction of minorities in S&E at every level of postsecondary education, with a progressive loss of representation as we move up the academic ladder.[4]

The Supreme Court's 1954 ruling in *Brown v. Board of Education* that segregation—the notion of separate but equal—in education was unconstitutional had provided an opportunity to transform the educational landscape in the United States. The civil rights movement over the subsequent two decades pushed for the integration in schools and colleges promised in *Brown* to become a reality. This hard work in the face of strong and even violent opposition yielded important results, as the percentage of African Americans over age twenty-five who have completed four or more years of college increased from 4 percent in the early 1960s to more than 20 percent today.[5]

However, challenges remain, particularly the very small numbers of African American doctorates in STEM fields relative to the 13 percent of the US population they comprise. In 2010 African Americans earning doctorates in STEM fields comprised only a very small number of the more than 57,000 research doctorates awarded by US institutions: 24 in mathematics, 33 in computer science, 80 in the physical sciences, 206 in the biological sciences, and 154 in engineering.[6] Given our history, these numbers are discouraging but not surprising: In 1975 African Americans earned just 1.2 percent of doctorates in the natural sciences, mathematics, and engineering. The percentage grew to 2.9 percent in 2000 and has since declined to 2.2 percent in 2010.

The National Academies committee argued that the United States must address this underrepresentation—and the corresponding waste of talent—for three reasons. First, it is the right thing to do for a society that believes in opportunity, social mobility, and fairness. Equity demands it. Second, we have for many years augmented our science and engineering talent pool by recruiting the best students and scholars from around the world. This strategy has yielded terrific results for the United States, but it is uncertain in a world increasingly characterized by global competition for talent, since many of these students may eventually return to their home countries. While the United States should continue to recruit the best talent worldwide, we must also focus on ensuring an adequate supply of US citizens from a population that will, by midcentury, include as many minorities as whites. If we do not include more minorities, our STEM workforce pipeline will weaken significantly. Finally, increasing demographic diversity also increases the range of research questions posed and the variety of perspectives about those questions. A workforce strategy that embraces equity and competitiveness also enriches our science and broadens research to include issues of importance to women, people of color, and low-income communities.

To address current underrepresentation in and the long-term strength of the US science and engineering workforce, the committee provided a set of recommendations that focus on practices from preschool through graduate school. However, we placed a priority on improving outcomes for underrepresented minorities who matriculate at four-year colleges and universities with an aspiration to complete a bachelor's degree in a STEM field. It was clear to us that the undergraduate years were a period during which the attrition of minority students was significant. The Higher Education Research Institute at the University of California, Los Angeles, found that African American, Hispanic American, and Native American students initially aspired to major in a STEM field at the same rates as white and Asian American students, but they were much less likely to have completed a bachelor's degree in one of these fields five years later.[7] At the same time, however, there had been enough successful experiments for increasing the participation and grad-uation of underrepresented minorities in undergraduate STEM majors that we had a body of research and a set of model programs we could draw on that would lay out very clearly how to address this issue. One of the models that informed the study was the Meyerhoff Program at UMBC.

ORIGINS OF THE MEYERHOFF PROGRAM

I started at UMBC as vice provost for academic affairs on April 1, 1987—April Fool's Day. So maybe I should have expected that I would be confronted with a critical challenge right at the start, and indeed, within the first week, I was. One morning when I arrived at my office on the tenth floor of the administration building, I found that the floor had been taken over by the Black Student Union. Among the black students assembled were some white students who were supporting them.

"What is the problem?" I asked. One black secretary on the floor responded, "Oh, don't worry. This happens every spring at UMBC." I thought, "Oh my God, what have I gotten myself into?" I had become "the man" (i.e., the administration). When I asked the students what they were protesting, they said, "Racism." I probed fur-ther, and different students cited a variety of examples of what appeared to them to represent racist behavior. For example, some said that when blacks and whites were in the same class, black students typically received lower grades than white students. Since the teacher was white, it must be racism. What else could it be?

Almost half of all four-year colleges and universities

in the United States, including most public institutions in Maryland, a southern state, were founded when education throughout the country was segregated.[8] When UMBC welcomed its first students in the fall of 1966, the law of the land in the post-*Brown* environment required that qualified students from all backgrounds could attend. So UMBC admitted both white and black students from its inception. Over the next two decades, UMBC enrolled a growing number of students, initially those primarily from the Baltimore area who otherwise would have attended the University of Maryland, College Park, and other Maryland institutions. The racial composition of the UMBC undergraduate population in the fall of 1985, about two decades later, was 78 percent white, 13 percent black, 6 percent Asian, and 3 percent other. (In 2013 UMBC was even more diverse, as undergraduate enrollment was 45 percent white, 16 percent black, 20 percent Asian, 6 percent Hispanic, 5 percent international, 4 percent two or more races, and 4 percent other.)[9]

While there were many faculty and staff who were supportive of our black students—about one out of every six students at the time—racial issues continued to be a challenge in the late 1980s. There were racial incidents and tensions among students. There were racial gaps in academic achievement that required further examination as well. Some black students at UMBC had been performing well in the social sciences and the humanities, disciplines that had produced a number of graduates who went on to law school. However, the performance of black students in the natural sciences was problematic. Very few students were succeeding in these disciplines and even fewer earned Bs in coursework. In fact, most were failing in these disciplines. To reach parity in achievement would require leadership, an examination of our practices, research on best practices for supporting minority students, additional external funding, and student and faculty buy-in. We had a lot of work to do.

LEADERSHIP, SELF-EXAMINATION, AND BEST PRACTICES

To effect a fundamental change in campus culture, a strong commitment from leadership is crucial to success. Senior campus leaders—president, provost, deans, and department chairs—must signal the importance of an issue and shape campus discussion on it through their direct involvement. In the case of UMBC, President Hooker, Provost Adam Yarmolinsky, and I as vice provost, along with a handful of faculty and staff colleagues, made the development of a program to support the academic success of African Americans in science a campus priority. Leadership signaled to our campus the importance of changing expectations so that high achievement for African Americans became first a goal and then a reality. In the years since, expectations have shifted dramatically as we have instilled a culture of "inclusive excellence" that celebrates high academic achievement for all our students, including African Americans. The faculty, who were accustomed to student failure, which they saw as the result of students' poor academic preparation, now embrace the notion that, with support, our students of all races can succeed.

Once leadership had signaled the importance of change, the crucial next step was to "look in the mirror" to better understand our current values, beliefs, and practices so that we could reshape them. In order to address a problem, one must first identify it by name, understand its dimensions, and then engage in discussions about how to determine the interests of key faculty and administrators in supporting new initiatives.[10]

As we grappled with the issues and the levers for addressing them, we dug deeper into the data on academic progress across racial groups at UMBC and were surprised by what we found. I had asked the black students, "How are you doing academically?" Every student said, "I'm fine academically. That's not the problem. It's just this environment." But when we examined the data on grade point averages, we saw a different picture: average GPAs for black students at UMBC were 1.9 for men and 2.0 for women. White students had higher GPAs and Asian Americans had the highest, but their GPAs were actually not so much higher that we were able to avoid the following conclusion: The best-prepared white and Asian students did fine in science, and many went on to medical school and became doctors, but large numbers of students of all races were not achieving what they had come to UMBC to achieve. Half of the black students were flunking out, and more than one-third of the white kids were, too. We needed to explore this problem more deeply and broadly if we were to strengthen student chances for success.

Faculty were committed to students, but we had two deep challenges that we had to confront in order to improve academic performance. First, we had not really taken a close look at the minimum level of preparation needed by students—of any race or ethnicity—to have a reasonable chance of making it at UMBC. We wanted to help everyone, so we were admitting a lot of students, but some of these students in the late 1980s did not have the background needed to succeed as undergraduates. Like many universities, we simply did not understand the relationship between the level of preparation of the students we admitted and the level of academic support we offered. In other words, many of the students actually needed more support than we could provide. Second, we as an institution—administration and faculty—had not talked adequately about our expectations for student success across racial groups and disciplines. For example, we went back to the data and could find almost no African Americans who had earned an A in any upper-level science course. When we spoke with faculty about this, they said, "Yes, we have had African Americans who have done well." However, in every case it turned out that the black student pointed to was from another country—Senegal, Nigeria, or the Caribbean—and they often had had an elite British or French education. When I first noted that, some blacks and whites, students and faculty, felt uncomfortable with my honesty. Blacks said, "Why would you embarrass us by saying something like that?" I argued that you can only address a problem if you first identify it. It was time to name the problem, change expectations, and take actions that would improve outcomes for students.

As we understood the issues more clearly, the next step was to understand what other institutions had done—and explore best practices to the extent they existed—to help formulate a set of actions, perhaps a program, that would test whether African Americans could succeed at a predominantly white institution in science and engineering. And so, I decided to look for predominantly white universities that graduated at least ten African American students per year who went on to complete PhDs in science and engineering. To my surprise, I could not find one. We did, however, draw on lessons learned from Uri Treisman's work with minority students in mathematics at the University of California, Berkeley. Treisman had developed the Mathematics Workshop at Berkeley in 1977 as a program for a diverse group of students—including African Americans—who were aggressively recruited for it. Later known as the Emerging Scholars Program, the initiative was not remedial but rather focused on academic success, defined as students' earning As and Bs in gateway mathematics courses and mastering the content so that they could succeed in advanced courses as well. Emerging Scholars communicated to participants the level of hard work needed for good mathematics students to become mathematicians, and then provided the support they needed to undertake that work. It provided a community for participating students that overcame the debilitating sense of isolation and discouragement many students felt in first-year mathematics courses when they were struggling with the material and without peer support.[11] My colleagues and I talked about the practical aspects of a program at UMBC that would use tutors and study groups the way the Berkeley Mathematics Workshop had. We talked about the importance of providing experiences that would make the students feel special. We talked about attracting really good students.

A practical approach to the issues—those we discovered by investigating the concerns of the black student protesters and exploring best practices—needed to be invented. The first step was to identify our goals. I said,

"Well, if many white students aren't making it at UMBC, and the academic preparation of black students is not as strong as that of whites, how can we possibly expect to get black students to succeed?" So I flipped our expectations. I decided to have what Jim Collins and Jerry Porras, authors of *Built to Last*, call "a big, hairy, audacious goal."[12] I said, "We don't want to just get black students to graduate. We want them to have done so well and to have had such a rich academic and social experience that they will have As and Bs in their major, they will have participated directly in research, and they will go on to graduate school and earn PhDs. We want these students to be the best in class." And then I said something that made people laugh: "One of our students will become the first black to win the Nobel Prize in Medicine or Science. You think I'm kidding, but I'm very serious." Blacks have won the Nobel Peace Prize and the Nobel Prize in Literature. These are amazing honors, and we are proud of the Nobel laureates who have won them. But we have not reached that level of achievement in medicine and science, and the time for this has come.

We not only wanted to attract the best African American students—the top such students from both predominantly black and integrated high schools in Maryland and, in later years, from around the nation—we also wanted them to work hard and succeed. About this time, we conducted an informal survey of the study habits of students and found that, in general, the Asian American students studied more than the white students, who in turn studied more than the black and Hispanic students. But the students from other countries studied the most, whether they were from Jamaica, Nigeria, Russia, India,

China, or anywhere else. As we began to have the conversations about our goals and approaches for supporting student success, this was an important lesson to keep in mind. For minority students to succeed, we needed to instill in them the same kind of values and hunger that you find in the immigrant experience. Many American Nobel laureates have been immigrants or the children of immigrants. They attended what was often referred to as the "poor man's Harvard," namely, City College or Brooklyn College, but rose to the very top of their fields. What made the difference? The excitement of being in the United States, the opportunities that lay before them, and the possibility of taking advantage of those opportunities through hard work.

As the Meyerhoff Program—which had evolved out of these conversations—developed over the years, we recognized that just as we had to instill hunger in our students, we had to change the culture of science, mathematics, and engineering education more broadly. At UMBC many black students were not making it in these fields, but neither were many white and Asian students—and the same could be said of students across the country. In fact, as the Meyerhoff Program developed and started showing significant gains, we began to hear white students at UMBC asking why they were not getting the support offered to the successful minority students enrolled as Meyerhoff Scholars. Eventually, the Meyerhoff Program was opened to students of all backgrounds.

The problem of academic culture affects students of all races and ethnic groups. Nationally, only about 20 percent of blacks and Hispanics who aspire to a major in science and engineering graduate with a degree in those fields, but the same is true for 32 percent of whites and 42 percent of Asian Americans.[13] Moreover, the higher a student's SAT scores, the larger the number of his or her Advanced Placement (AP) credits, and the more prestigious the college or university that the student attends, the greater the probability that a student who starts in science and engineering will leave it within the first year.[14] Once when I talked about these data at a federal agency, the agency's general counsel said to me afterwards, "You just told my story. I was valedictorian of my high school class, I had perfect SAT scores, and I went to one of the most prestigious universities. I started off in premed, got a C in chemistry and an A in my humanities courses, and I went home and told people, 'I love the humanities and I'm changing my major.' So I became a lawyer. I had always thought my own poor performance in science was the problem." But the point was that she, along with many others who could have succeeded in science, left because the culture had not supported and encouraged her.

One reason for this attrition, traditionally, has been that the undergraduate classes in these fields are not nurturing; indeed, the first-year classes tend to be just the opposite, serving as "weed-out courses." Too few institutions have worked on redesigning courses to consider new methods of teaching that complement the traditional lecture method. Many institutions do not encourage students to work in groups or to seek help, which often leaves them fending for themselves when they might benefit from group work or tutoring. In addition, some of the highest-achieving students are encouraged to start with advanced classes in mathematics and science, and many of these students do not compete well with more experienced students. Accustomed to performing at the highest levels, they are discouraged by their relatively poor performance and switch out of science and engineering. I often ask institutions if they have attempted to understand and address this attrition—too few have looked at data. Ultimately, it is the expectation in many science and engineering departments that a large proportion of students will change their majors; we can see that the number of seats allotted for these disciplines is reduced in the second year. Most institutions don't anticipate that all or even most students will continue in these fields, and this tends to become a self-fulfilling prophecy.

We decided that our strategy would be this: we would bring in the best African American students we could recruit and support them through a "strengths-based" program. Rather than a deficits-based approach that focuses on remediating deficiencies in student preparation, we would recruit talented, prepared students and build on their existing strengths through high expectations and a transformative academic and social environment.[15] As my colleague Ken Maton and I have noted in an article describing the Meyerhoff Program, recent research has confirmed the assumptions underlying our program, concluding that among those African Americans who aspire to a bachelor's degree with a major in a STEM field but do not earn one—underperforming in science and quantitative courses—are students with high standardized test scores, impressive high school grades, and participation in high school honors math and science courses.[16] This research, we observed, has also identified "factors other than precollegiate preparation and native ability that work to depress minority achievement and persistence" in college, and that these factors "include academic and cultural isolation, motivation and performance vulnerability in the face of negative stereotypes and low expectations, peers who are not supportive of academic success, and perceived and actual discrimination."[17] A program built on student strengths, and providing financial, academic, and social support, creates the opportunity for success.

CREATING A PROGRAM

We had developed a better understanding of the issues and had determined priorities on which to focus, but we did not yet have a plan to move forward. About this time, in 1988, Robert Embry, president of the Abell Foundation and former Baltimore City school board president, discovered that two friends of his had a common concern. He knew that I wanted to improve the success of African Americans in mathematics and science at UMBC. He also knew that Robert Meyerhoff, a Baltimore philanthropist, had been talking about the need to improve the lives of black males—remarking, for example, that everything he saw on TV about young black men was negative except when it came to sports—and he was trying to figure out how he could contribute to positive change. So Bob Embry suggested that I call Robert Meyerhoff. Since UMBC president Michael Hooker had encouraged me to do whatever we could to get people involved in supporting us, I was very excited to meet Mr. Meyerhoff in what was to be the most important, transformational moment of my career.

Robert Meyerhoff and I initiated a series of conversations. I sensed his authenticity immediately. He wanted to make a difference, and he specifically said, "I care about all young people, but nobody wants to deal with this issue that black males are at the bottom, when you look at who is put out of school all the time, when you look at who is in jail." I talked about the poor performance of black students in science, mathematics, and engineering fields on campus. He asked for a brief proposal describing the vision for a program that would educate black male students in these disciplines. He said, "I want the country to understand that if you support black males they can do as well as anybody else, if not better." It was very powerful to have someone of his stature commit to this goal.

Back at UMBC, I went about developing a $500,000 proposal outlining a program that drew on my personal and professional experiences, the suggestions of my colleagues, and the examples of such successful programs as Treisman's Emerging Scholars Program. I took the proposal back to Bob Meyerhoff, and I waited while he read it, thinking, "I asked for half a million dollars, but it would be great if he gave even $100,000." At one point he stopped reading and looked at me, and began asking a number of penetrating questions. It was clear that he took our proposal seriously. He then had me talk with his attorney, who asked further tough questions, probing to determine the feasibility of the program we were proposing. I was impressed by the rigorous questioning—clearly Mr. Meyerhoff was interested in the concept and willing to provide funding, but he wanted to make sure the program could produce results. Once we addressed his questions, he said, "I like this. You got it." I said, "Got what?"

He said, "You got the half million." My head was swimming. That was a lot of money in 1988.

I then had the nerve to ask, "But could we expand the program to include women? We at UMBC want to help women too." Bob and Jane Meyerhoff had already been providing support for women's programs—for example, at Goucher College in Baltimore. For this project, he reaffirmed his desire to focus on supporting black men. Bob Meyerhoff has not merely provided funding for the program that bears his name over a quarter century; he has taken a personal interest in the students, often relating stories of their challenges and successes.

It was especially courageous of Bob to focus on the challenges of black males at a time when many people were uncomfortable addressing the problems of this group. (Twenty-five years later, in 2014, President Barack Obama brought the challenges of black males back to the nation's attention with the "My Brother's Keeper" initiative.) The Meyerhoff Program, as it came to be called, thus began with black men in its first cohort, although we did add black women in the second year, and then, with time, women and men of all races.[18] The key criterion for admission, in addition to high achievement in mathematics and science, was that students had to demonstrate an interest in the mission of the program, namely, to increase the number of underrepresented minority students participating and succeeding in STEM.

The reactions to the initial focus on men were divergent. On the one hand, those most excited about having a program for black men were the parents of black women. They said, "We need more young men who can step up to the plate." Thus, we had their strong support. A national women's organization, however, argued that the program was biased toward men and therefore discriminatory. I appreciated their concern and understood their perspective. However, they did not fully understand how gender dynamics in the black community differed from those in the mainstream. Most notably, African American women were actually making more progress than men in higher education, as their college enrollments were growing much faster. We had a conversation about these dynamics, and the organization's leadership came to understand the rationale behind our approach.

CELEBRATING "THE BEST": STUDENT AND FAMILY BUY-IN

With funding in hand and the establishment of a new program, our next step was to recruit potential students by getting them and their parents excited about the opportunities that our new program would provide. In 1989 we began our recruitment efforts by seeking the most academically prepared students we could find. We viewed the future scientists we would be educating as one component of the black leadership (the "talented tenth") that W. E. B. Du Bois described in the early twentieth century. They would become the future professors and researchers, as well as administrators, mentors, and respected community leaders. We had a duty to nurture these future professionals who, as role models, teachers, researchers, and policymakers, would have an important impact on African American and other students and directly contribute to the well-being and vitality of American society generally.

We were, of course, immediately challenged on this

approach by many who heard about it. Almost everyone said, "Why are you starting with the best-prepared kids? You are just skimming the cream off the top!" Others argued that in light of the crippling poverty facing many black families and the underperformance of African American students in the public schools, we should focus on raising the education levels of African Americans more generally rather than targeting scarce resources to support African Americans who were already high-achieving. But our position was that these approaches were not mutually exclusive, that both could and should be undertaken simultaneously, that even high-achieving black students could be enabled and inspired to do better if properly supported. We were in an excellent position to provide that support so that the highest achievers would have the best shot at becoming leaders in the American STEM community, positions from which they themselves could help other high achievers and work to raise the education levels of African American students overall. In addition, what most Americans did not know was that the majority of high-achieving black students were not excelling in STEM disciplines in college, and this was an outcome we wanted and needed to change.

As a first step, we invited to campus a group of students we believed would be strong candidates for our new program. We had contacted school principals, guidance counselors, and science and mathematics teachers at both predominantly black and integrated high schools across Maryland asking them to recommend their top African American male students in their senior year. Most of these students and their families were looking at Amer-

ica's most prestigious universities, which posed a challenge for us as we launched our program. We asked them
to come to our campus for a "Meyerhoff Weekend"—a
notable opportunity for African American male students
to discuss college opportunities and meet the other top
black students from Maryland who would be there. During the weekend we discussed the significance of being
a young, gifted African American man in science, the
challenges that African American men face in high
school and college (both in general and specifically in
science and engineering), and how the Meyerhoff Program would work to prepare students to become PhD researchers. Most students and their parents saw medicine
or engineering—not research—as the goal, so we focused
on the importance of PhD researchers and what these
professionals could do, for example, to address health disparities. Lastly, the students learned how the program we
had created would work and the kind of scholarships we
could offer.[19]

The focus on health disparities was particularly powerful for these students and their families. In our Meyerhoff Weekends, Dr. Michael Summers, a Howard Hughes
Medical Institute (HHMI) investigator at UMBC and
one of our program mentors, tells the participants the following:

> I would like you to take a careful look at your mother,
> if you came here with her. Now take a look at your
> father:
>
> > If your father is African American, his risk of dying
> > of high blood pressure is 350 percent greater than
> > that of his white friends.

If your mother is African American, her risk is 300 percent greater.

If your parents are African American, their risk of developing hypertension is 200 percent greater than that of whites.

If your mother is African American, there is a one in four chance that she will develop diabetes by the time she is fifty.

African American women are three times more likely to develop lupus.

Consider the fact that sickled red blood cells were discovered near the turn of the twentieth century, but it was nearly fifty years before the first penny of federal funds was spent to study the disease.

Who do you expect to address these issues? Who will do the research or make the funding decisions? You will be among the brightest students in your class when you go to college, and you will have the opportunity to do more than just put Band-Aids on problems. You will have the opportunity to find cures.

The discussion provoked by these questions is very powerful.

Most students who came to campus for the first Meyerhoff Weekend were not accustomed to being part of a large group of gifted African American male students who had excelled in advanced, rigorous mathematics and science courses. Particularly in integrated high schools, they were more accustomed to being the "only one" in these courses. Having them all in one room, building on the energy one could feel in the group as they gathered, was a watershed moment for them and for us and provided an important opportunity to begin a process that would take their current values of hard work and excellence and shape even stronger values, self-identities, and dreams. African American men are subject to strong stereotypes in American culture—negatively portrayed in the context of violence at worst, or positively portrayed in the context of sports at best. We in the Meyerhoff Program experienced this firsthand. When the Meyerhoff Program staff took the first cohort of nineteen men on trips, onlookers' first reactions—for example, in a restaurant or a church—was that this must be UMBC's basketball team. We often found ourselves explaining that these were some of the best students on campus and were part of an academic program for gifted science majors. So it was critical to promote high expectations for these students, and the first opportunity to do so presented itself during the first Meyerhoff Weekend.[20]

At one point during the weekend, we asked each student to walk up onto a stage and talk about himself: his name, where he was from, one achievement of which he was particularly proud, and his dream. As each student came across the stage, not one of them mentioned an academic achievement. They were too embarrassed to do so. Instead, they talked about being in the band or being a wrestler or something else related to sports. When I realized what was happening, I told the group to prepare to come across the stage again and this time to name one academic achievement of which they were proud. The first young man to return to the stage attended Baltimore Polytechnic Institute, a Baltimore City high school, once all-white and now largely black. At the time, though, Poly—as it is familiarly known—still had many middle-class white kids among its students, and this student said he was about to become valedictorian. He came across the stage and said, with embarrassment, "I have never made a B." He had his head down. And it hit me. I said, "Boy, come back here." Then I said to the whole group, "Do you all understand what he's telling you? This young man is telling you that he has earned As all his life." I turned back to the young man and said, "Son, let me tell you something. You're more special than you realize. I want you to say your name, and I want you to shout it out that you are a straight A student." He was still too quiet that second time, and so I said, "Say it again." The third time he shouted it out, and the room erupted—all of the visiting students and their families gave him a standing ovation. There were tears. It was a revelation. We, as a society, were not getting children excited about being smart, about wanting to be the best. Since then, the Meyerhoff Program has incorporated many practices like this to recognize and celebrate academic victories.

The first Meyerhoff Weekend was a stunning success: nineteen of the twenty-five young men who came to campus that weekend enrolled at UMBC and formed the first Meyerhoff cohort. We developed language to talk about high expectations for and the success of African American men, providing for these students what is so often taken for granted by their white counterparts. As this cohort moved through the program and demonstrated its success, we were able to talk about this success to new classes of students who, along with their parents, began to realize that the Meyerhoff Program was the only one of its kind for African Americans within a predominantly white institution. Soon, interest in the program grew steadily, reaching more than two thousand nominations to the program annually by 2012.

THE LAST INGREDIENT: FACULTY BUY-IN

As my colleagues and I developed the Meyerhoff Program, we found that faculty buy-in—and faculty leadership in discussions—was critical. In the early development of the program, while we were "looking in the mirror" to better understand UMBC and its students, we asked faculty the question, "Can high-achieving black students succeed in science and engineering at UMBC? What will it take?" Some of my colleagues who were well-meaning expressed grave concern about a program for minority students. First, they believed that such a program would be unfair to other students. Our approach to addressing this situation was to have conversations with faculty colleagues about the performance of different groups in the sciences. The data clearly showed that black students were not succeeding in science fields. Second, some colleagues had related concerns that some of the students to be recruited would not have the high school background necessary to succeed in science or engineering at UMBC. My response was that it would be worthwhile to consider the Meyerhoff Program an experiment and that we would be learning if it was possible to educate a substantial number of black students who would not simply survive in the sciences but excel. If we were successful, our intention was to identify practices that could be used to support students of all racial backgrounds. That is exactly what happened.

We brought faculty into problem solving with us to allow them to better understand the problem of minority achievement, become a part of the solution, and buy in to the new program. As it became a success, it provided an opportunity to also change the culture of the university. We have focused on teaching students how to work in groups and we have developed ways to increase faculty-student interaction through research. Most important, at the undergraduate and graduate levels, we use focus groups to aid faculty who seek to learn more about the perceptions and experiences of students. Often the focus groups lead to changes in practices within departments. The emphasis on assessment helps programs and faculty to make changes as necessary in their approaches to teaching.

Many key faculty helped to establish the Meyerhoff Program and raise and address elements in science education that improved instruction for both the Meyerhoff Scholars and undergraduate science majors generally. For example, the chair of our chemistry department at the time, Catherine Fenselau, had been a professor in the medical school at Johns Hopkins University. She played a critical role in focusing our efforts on improving the performance of undergraduates generally as well as talented minorities who had the potential to succeed in science. One of her important insights was that at the medical school almost every student admitted eventually completed the degree. That was the culture. In undergraduate science programs that allowed gateway courses to "weed out" students, she noted, there was a culture of acceptance that most students would not make it. For student success, this culture had to change.

We have sought to capture the notion of inclusive excellence—high achievement for students of all backgrounds—and the importance of faculty involvement in fostering it, on the cover of this book, which features Professor Michael Summers and two of his students. The vast majority of professors in research universities have been white men, with very few students of color achieving at the top. At the core of our success has been the important role of research professors embracing the vision of inclusive excellence in science and engineering. In a rapidly changing global society, students must learn to compete against and work with people from all over the world.

Dr. Mike Summers is a Howard Hughes Medical Institute (HHMI) investigator and professor of chemistry and biochemistry at UMBC who has been deeply involved in the Meyerhoff Program, bringing high-quality academic work and, therefore, a sense of legitimacy to the program, particularly in the eyes of other faculty. He has mentored many minority and international undergraduate and graduate students in his laboratory, which explores the structures of retroviruses, including HIV-1. Faculty like Mike have been indispensable to the success of the Meyerhoff Scholars Program, connecting teaching and learning to research that has been central to our program and that supports the success of high-achieving minorities in STEM fields. Other faculty have been enormously important to our success as well, and once we had their buy-in, we had committed faculty who taught science or engineering, made it a goal to work for the success of the students, pulled those students into their laboratories, and then helped them grow as scientist and engineers. Without this buy-in, the program would not have been the success for the students that it has been.

The students pictured on the cover are Ae Lim Yang and Sayo McCowin. Ae Lim was born in Seoul, South Korea, came to the United States with her family at age eleven, and graduated from Atholton High School in Columbia, Maryland. At the time of publication, Ae Lim was a sophomore in UMBC's Honors College and an affiliate in the Meyerhoff Scholars Program, majoring in biochemistry and molecular biology. She is also director of Service and Community Outreach for UMBC's Student Government Association. In Dr. Summers's lab, Ae Lim has been investigating simian immunodeficiency viruses (SIV) in chimpanzees, with an eye toward understanding their structural biology and how they are related to the viral evolution of HIV. Sayo attended Washington-Lee High School in Arlington, Virginia, and is currently a junior. At UMBC, he is a Meyerhoff Scholar with support from the Howard Hughes Medical Institute and the National Institute on Drug Abuse at the National Institutes of Health. He is majoring in biochemistry and biological sciences. His research in Dr. Summers's lab has focused on the structural biology of HIV-1, with a specific emphasis on CA-NC polyprotein and its role in genome recognition. Sayo just gave a poster presentation entitled "Mechanism of HIV-1 Capsid-Nucleocapsid Polyprotein in Genome Recognition" at the Annual Biomedical Research Conference for Minority Students (ABRCMS) in San Antonio, Texas. Both Ae Lim and Sayo hope to pursue the MD-PhD after graduation.

ELEMENTS OF THE MEYERHOFF PROGRAM

The Meyerhoff Scholars Program has evolved into a comprehensive, multicomponent program that addresses the range of factors associated with minority-student achievement in science and engineering. The elements of this program include excellent staff, institutional commitment, faculty involvement, academic support, social integration, financial support, and professional development.[21]

> *Program staff:* The program—and the participating students—have benefited from excellent staff, who have provided leadership for the effort, guidance, and support for the students, and management for the program. Barbara Uncle helped in writing the first Meyerhoff proposal. Susan Boyer, Earnestine Baker, Lamont Tolliver, and Keith Harmon have served as the four directors of the program since its inception.

> *Institutional commitment:* Institutional commitment is crucial for the success of an experiment, which the Meyerhoff Program was when we admitted the first cohort of nineteen African American men in 1989. This commitment from the institution begins at the top, with a dedication to the program from the administration itself, and relies on an active effort from the administration and the faculty to create a culture throughout the university that emphasizes diversity, excellence, and success, a culture based on nurturing students who bring a great deal of talent to the table. The commitment is demonstrated with the recruitment process—and Meyerhoff Weekend—and

continues as the university leadership works to raise funding for the program, supervises program staff, and interacts with Meyerhoff Scholars periodically throughout the school year.

Faculty involvement: It takes researchers to produce researchers, so the involvement of faculty—most of whom are not minorities—is critically important. Indeed, as noted above, without faculty buy-in, the program would not succeed. Faculty teach, advise, mentor, provide research opportunities in their laboratories, and support students as they apply to graduate and professional school programs.

Recruitment: The critical factor in selecting students is deciding how strong a background a student needs to have a reasonable chance of succeeding. We look first at traditional measures such as grades and test scores, with a particular focus on mathematics and reading skills. But those are not the only factors that matter. When we see a high school student from an inner-city school who has a math SAT score in the 600s, strong As and Bs, and the right attitude, we can often help that student do as well as a student from a suburban school with a substantially higher math score. Attitude makes all the difference in the world: a demonstrated ability to work hard and persevere. Each year we admit applicants to UMBC who are promising students but not competitive for the Meyerhoff Program. We tell them, "If you come here, work with the Meyerhoff Program, earn at least a B in STEM courses, we will admit you into the program in your sophomore year." You would be surprised how many students who did not have stellar test scores and grades, who may not have worked as hard in high school as they might have, come to UMBC, begin to put in four, five, or six hours daily studying, build up their skills, and earn the grades needed to become affiliates of the Meyerhoff Scholars program in their sophomore years. In 2013, for example, thirteen students did so.

Academic support: Academic support begins with a six-week residential summer-bridge program. We realized early on that we could not take minority students—even high-achieving students—who came from a wide variety of academic and social cultures, and expect them to immediately assimilate to UMBC's. We had to create a deliberate process through which they got to know one another, our faculty, and our campus culture. We also had to prepare them for just how much work was going to be required of them if they were going to excel. Even though they were high achieving, they were going to have a hard time competing academically with white or Asian students from Montgomery County, Maryland, or international students from Russia or China, who comfortably earned 800s on the mathematics SAT and 5s on AP exams in the tenth grade.

The question was how to give students from traditionally underrepresented groups an equal footing. And so the bridge program is not only a bridge but also an academic boot camp. It shakes students up in many ways. It is a highly scheduled, intensive program that includes two academic courses (one in mathematics and one in general education), supplemental instruction including skills seminars, and site visits to research laboratories. It includes academic advising, tutoring, and personal counseling that then continue throughout the program. It introduces students to the importance of group study, a feature of the program that emerged from my own educational experiences. Most high-achieving high school students are not accustomed to working in groups. Typically, students have received the message in elementary and high school that when they work together they are cheating. Moreover, they have generally performed well working by themselves. In fact, they will tell you, "I don't need anybody else." The more enlightened approach, however, is to understand that whether one is working in the humanities, social sciences, natural sciences, or engineering, we all learn more by asking questions and interacting with each other in groups. All of these elements—advising, tutoring, and group study—continue through the Meyerhoff Scholars' undergraduate experience.

Undergraduate research: Involving students in research—which requires faculty involvement—is also a critical component of the Meyerhoff Program, which requires students to gain research experience. To become a scientist or engineer—and strongly identify as one—requires "doing the science" or "doing the engineering"; that is, taking the knowledge learned in the classroom and applying it and becoming skilled at using the knowledge in the laboratory or in other practical settings. This experience allows students to reinforce the knowledge and feel the kind of self-efficacy as a scientist or engineer that is necessary for a successful career in STEM.

Social integration: The social aspects of the program are among its most powerful, providing students with a sense of community that overcomes any potential sense of isolation, increases student identification with the program, and serves to support the group work that is also important for academic success.

This social integration begins during the summer bridge program between high school and freshman year, during which we begin to cultivate in the students an identity as a Meyerhoff Scholar and a sense of belonging to the "Meyerhoff family." We also begin to instill values that will shape their experience as "a Meyerhoff" and, we hope, their entire lives. These include high academic expectations, a belief that excellence demands hard work and sacrifice, a sense of responsibility and accountability to themselves and to their peers, and a commitment to group success. We encourage the students to sit in the front of the classroom, ask questions, get to know faculty and staff (in part, to identify people who can serve as references for summer internships and admissions to doctoral programs), take advantage of group study and tutoring, develop a strong support group with students who are serious about studying, and relate their experiences from research and internships to their coursework. We teach them to identify their strengths and weaknesses, develop self-motivation and a thick skin, and seek constructive criticism. Finally, we encourage the students to envision completing a PhD in science or engineering as a career goal and commit to supporting diversity in STEM fields. We encourage the students to reflect on what it means to be both high-achieving and minority in American society. What are the challenges, opportunities, and responsibilities that these imply?

We make a great effort to foster a sense of community. During the summer bridge program, we now take away students' cell phones and computers. This was an idea that developed over time from listening to the students. In the early years of the Meyerhoff Program, we found that students were not building community in that summer bridge experience because they were spending more time with their friends in other places, through technology, than they were getting to know the people in the same room. Our goal is to have them bond like a family, because the stronger that community is, the stronger each person would be.

We also foster a sense of community during the entire undergraduate experience by requiring Meyerhoff Scholars to live on campus all four years, live in the same residence hall as their Meyerhoff cohort during the summer bridge and freshman year, and participate in meetings of their cohort and the larger Meyerhoff family. That family includes all of the Meyerhoff cohorts, past and present, the faculty and staff involved in the program, and parents. We hold a dinner at the end of each academic year to celebrate the success of the graduating Meyerhoff cohort that focuses on the work they have done and their plans for the future, which typically includes graduate school. Active parental involvement is also key. Parents participate in social events, are expected to consistently encourage their kids, and become partners in problem solving when students are not doing well.

A final social aspect of the program is service. We encourage our students to be proud to be a Meyerhoff and to be known as smart, but we also say to them, "To whom much is given much is required." So service plays a key role in both character development and social cohesion. It helps to develop students as leaders who can help other people who also have struggles to overcome. For example, we encourage them to engage in extracurricular community service such as tutoring low-income children, which promotes their emotional and intellectual development. One readily available opportunity is to volunteer in the Choice Program, run through UMBC's Shriver Center. This program provides supervision twenty-four hours a day, seven days a week to young first-time criminal offenders, often black and Latino boys. Through this program, Meyerhoff students can engage with these children, serving as mentors and providing them an opportunity to reflect on how difficult the life of a black boy in poverty can be, how fortunate they themselves are, and what role educated blacks may play in helping poor children.[22]

Financial support: The Meyerhoff Program provides substantial scholarship support. We provide scholarships, first, as a way of recognizing and developing talent. The students earn the scholarships by showing their potential during the application process. We provide them also because we want the students and their families to be able to afford an excellent education. And we provide this support because we want the students to focus on academics. I like to say, "In order to succeed in biochemistry, you can't be a part-time friend. You have to marry the work." That is, a student who works off-campus twenty hours per week is not going to make it in mathematics, science, or engineering. He or she needs to be in class, doing homework, and working in the lab. That is the only way they will earn the As and Bs that will allow them to move confidently to higher levels and, eventually, go on to graduate school.

Professional development for students: All of this focus on the academics is reinforced through professional-development activities. Through the Meyerhoff Program, students are provided with mentoring, designed to inform and guide them toward academic and career goals. As noted above, the undergraduate research experience is a key academic component of the program. This occurs in labs during the school year, but in addition, Meyerhoff Scholars are required to do research or take a class during the summer, a requirement that is important for both their academic and professional development. Summer research internships are typically set up with government agencies, private companies, or academic laboratories where the student will both learn through the work and, over the course of their undergraduate years, gain exposure to a variety of professional environments.

PROGRAM EVALUATION

A terrific outcome of the Meyerhoff Program for our own campus has been a culture of innovation that has led to a willingness to look in the mirror, identify problems, and take risks to find solutions. We have taken what we have learned through the Meyerhoff Program to develop similar scholars programs (in the humanities, public affairs, STEM teaching, and cybersecurity). We have also extended what has worked in the Meyerhoff Program to students across the campus through efforts such as course redesign across the sciences, engineering, humanities, and arts. We know what works because we developed a culture of evaluation that allows us to assess, through data analytics, whether our innovations are working and then make changes based on the data.

Shortly after the program began, I sought guidance in evaluating the early implementation of the Meyerhoff Program by inviting Dr. Willie Pearson, professor of sociology at Wake Forest University at the time (now professor in the School of History, Technology, and Society at the Georgia Institute of Technology), to visit UMBC. Dr. Pearson reaffirmed the importance of conducting research at every stage of the program's development. He then helped initiate our evaluation efforts, which led to our coauthored paper, "Recruiting and Retaining Talented African American Males in College Science and Engineering."[23] Building on that initial work with Dr. Pearson and with funding from the Alfred P. Sloan Foundation, I then began working with Dr. Ken Maton, professor of psychology at UMBC, who has led our research team examining the Meyerhoff Program for well over twenty years.

Since the Meyerhoff Program's inception, therefore, its components, strengths and weaknesses, and results have been the focus of continual, rigorous, and regularly published process and outcome evaluations conducted by various research groups—combining qualitative and quantitative assessment. Our research has led to two books, coauthored by Ken Maton, Geoffrey Greif, Monica Greene, and me, on raising academically successful African American students in science (on men and women, respectively).[24] We have also written numerous book chapters and articles, published in journals ranging from the *Journal of Research in Science Teaching* and the *Journal of College Science Teaching* to *American Psychologist* and the *Journal of Women and Minorities in Science and Engineering*.[25]

Process-evaluation data have been collected at various times, in various formats, and from multiple subgroups of African American Meyerhoff Scholars regarding their experiences in both the university overall and the Meyerhoff Program in particular. The primary purpose of this exercise has been to identify the factors perceived by students to be most important, and also to identify any negative aspects. Analysis of the data has shown six factors to be especially important:[26]

1. *Community:* Students consistently rate being part of the Meyerhoff community as a key program component. African American students felt less isolated than their peers who are not in the program and valued how it provides ready-made opportunities to form study groups.

2. *Financial support:* The availability of scholarship support allows students to focus on academics, without the distraction of off-campus work. This ability to focus results in enhanced academic performance, which then feeds into greater self-esteem.

3. *Program staff:* Meyerhoff Scholars consistently identify the work of the staff as important to their success. Staff are available to provide both academic advising and personal encouragement.

4. *Research:* Scholars consistently rate summer research experiences as important, as these provide them access to leading researchers, opportunities to learn, and a desire to pursue the PhD.

5. *Campus academic environment:* Scholars also speak positively about the campus academic culture, which they have, in a way, played a strong role in creating. Faculty report that the performance of Meyerhoff Scholars has greatly influenced faculty's perceptions of the capability of African American students. That improved perception, in turn, has helped to create the improved academic climate for African Americans at UMBC, and this goes on to benefit future Meyerhoff cohorts. Meyerhoff participants, compared to students who declined the scholarship and matriculated elsewhere, report lower levels of stress in their interactions with faculty.

6. *Professional development:* Scholars report significantly greater opportunities for networking than students not in the program, capitalizing on summer research and other experiences.

Equally important have been our outcome-evaluation efforts that have involved assessing the performance of the African American Meyerhoff Scholars against the performance of two comparison groups of students: one group, the "historical" sample, included comparably talented African American STEM majors who attended UMBC before the program was launched in 1989; the second group, the "declined" sample, included African American students who were admitted to the program but chose instead to attend other institutions.

Meyerhoff Scholars significantly outperformed both groups. Whereas students in the "historical" sample had significantly lower GPAs in science courses than their white and Asian American counterparts, Meyerhoff Scholars' GPAs were comparable or higher. Compared to students in the "declined" sample, Meyerhoff Scholars were nearly twice as likely to persist and graduate in science and engineering undergraduate majors, achieved significantly higher GPAs in science and engineering courses, and were more than five times more likely to complete science and engineering PhDs or MD-PhDs. Today, many Meyerhoff Scholars who have completed graduate school now hold faculty positions at prestigious universities in the Ivy League, the Big Ten, and elsewhere.[27]

To ensure that we have met our goals of educating

minority students who go on to earn the PhD, we have also compared our outcomes to those of other universities by analyzing data from the National Science Foundation that track students from their undergraduate programs through the doctorate. Based on this analysis, we have found that:

- UMBC was the number 8 baccalaureate-origin institution for black students who went on to complete a PhD in the natural sciences or engineering from 2002 to 2011. From 2007 to 2011, UMBC moved up to number 6, and we expect to continue to rise in the rankings.

- UMBC ranked as the number 2 baccalaureate-origin institution, behind Xavier University, for blacks completing a PhD in the biological sciences from 2007 to 2011.

- UMBC was the number 1 predominantly white institution whose black undergraduates earned the PhD in the natural sciences or engineering from 2002 to 2011.

Since historically black universities have a much larger population of black students who could go on to graduate school, we also analyzed the data on a per capita basis. We found that the Massachusetts Institute of Technology (MIT) had the highest percentage of its black undergraduates go on to earn PhDs in the natural sciences and engineering. UMBC was second, followed by Princeton, Johns Hopkins, Yale, Brown, and Georgia Tech.[28]

Our goal is to produce large numbers of leaders in STEM fields with the understanding that they will make significant contributions in their fields, leading to tenured positions in academia, research positions in industry, and one day prestigious honors, including becoming HHMI investigators or even winning the Nobel Prize in Medicine. So there have been terrific outcomes for our students, of whom we are very proud. Based on this success, there are now two substantial efforts to fully replicate the Meyerhoff Program elsewhere, at Pennsylvania State University and the University of North Carolina at Chapel Hill. Many other campuses, including Duke, Cornell, Michigan, Colby, Morehouse, and Winston-Salem, have adapted components of our program to diversity programs of their own.

CONCLUSION

After the Meyerhoff Program had been launched and we began recruiting many of the best-prepared African Americans in science and engineering, I had the occasion to visit one of our nation's leading research universities. I will never forget this visit, because it reinforced for me the importance of our work. In the course of the visit, I met with the university's provost along with all of his deans, almost all of whom were white men (there may have been one woman and one Hispanic). They were wonderful to me personally, but as a group they said, "You're attracting students to UMBC who were going to come to our university." The provost asked, "How can you justify that?" I said, "Quite easily, because if they had come to you they never would have made it. And even if they had made it, most would complete a bachelor's degree in engineering and then say, 'I don't ever want to see it again in my life. I'm going to law school or business.' The reason for that is that you don't value the nurturing of students here."

My colleagues and I have been on a mission since the late 1980s. And we have had success. Since the inception of the Meyerhoff Program, more than 200 graduates who have gone on to earn the PhD or MD-PhD, more than 100 have earned an MD, nearly 250 have earned a master's degree, and more than 300 are currently enrolled in a graduate or professional degree program.

The reason we have had success is that we have focused on nurturing—indeed, this is not just a "program" but rather a deep interaction with the students that simultaneously pushes them, embraces them, and supports them. For success, you have to know the students and connect with them personally. You have to want to help them want to be smart, to be passionate about the work, and to dream.

4

Raising a Generation of Achievers

A CULTURE OF SUCCESS IN STEM EDUCATION

When speaking around the country, I often give people the following sixth-grade math problem:

> Twenty-nine children are in a class. Twenty have dogs. Fifteen have cats. How many have both a dog and a cat?

Take a moment to think about it.[1]

People approaching the problem tend to fall into one of three groups. Those who were successful in math at school immediately begin working to solve the problem in their heads. Others who struggled with math as children wonder, "Why is he giving us a math problem?" and don't even try to figure it out. And the final group is in the middle: they're willing to try to solve the problem but aren't confident they will arrive at the right answer. These three responses mirror those you'll find in any sixth-grade class or college seminar.

While audiences are pondering the math problem, I ask them how many love math. I often see only a smattering of hands. Even among highly educated Americans, few express a love for math; sometimes I'm even asked, "How can you put *love* and *math* in the same sentence?"

Our attitudes in this country are such that we tend to think that math and science are just for a few smart people, and our educational system encourages most people to sort themselves *out* of the STEM fields early on. By the time American students enter high school, they are certain of whether they are a math and science type, a history and English type, or an arts type. How do they know that at such a young age? I am convinced that we tell young children—based on their enthusiasm or how quickly they grasp certain concepts—that they are either a math and science type or they are not. When they hear that message often enough, they come to believe it. Such early typecasting of students, based on a very narrow and entirely inaccurate view of what it means to have an aptitude for STEM subjects, prevents children from developing an identity as a "STEM person." Many of those kids, in fact, have a great aptitude for science, technology, engineering, and math, and—if nurtured and supported—could go on to successful, productive careers in those fields.

How can we change that fundamental attitude? We must change the culture of our schools to stop typecasting students at a young age. And colleges and universities must find a better way to support the students who do arrive at their doors interested in STEM. Far too many are not making it.

While typecasting and "weeding out" is particularly common around STEM fields, it in fact happens across disciplines and at all levels of education. How many of you have heard someone say of a young student—maybe a fifth or sixth grader—that he or she isn't "college material"? And that thinking does not stop once a student has actually made it to college. As a college freshman in 1966, I remember the convocation speaker saying to our class, "Look to your left; look to your right; one of you will not graduate." At UMBC, we say, "Look to your left; look to your right; our goal is to make sure all of you graduate. If you don't, we've failed—and we're not planning to fail." We must show that same kind of commitment across the educational spectrum if we are to help more Americans build better lives, while also enhancing the country's competitive edge.

Over the last five decades, the percentage of Americans with a bachelor's degree or higher has tripled. In the mid-1960s, just 10 percent of American adults had four-year college degrees, while today, more than 30 percent—nearly one in three—do.[2] But while it's true that more Americans than ever hold college degrees, young Americans are falling behind their peers in a significant, and growing, number of countries in degree attainment. American adults overall are the second-most-educated group of people in the world, behind only Norwegians for bachelor's-degree attainment. But younger Americans, those twenty-five to thirty-four years old, rank twelfth globally, behind their peers in eleven other countries including the United Kingdom, Australia, Japan, and Poland.[3] For the first time since the middle of the twentieth century, we cannot say that each generation of Americans will be more educated than the generation before it.

At the same time as our educational standing is slipping among countries with developed economies, rapid gains are being made in both technology and education by new competitors. In response to the emergence of China, India, and several other countries as global competitors, the Obama administration has ratcheted up its educational goals, aiming to increase the percentage of American adults having two- and four-year degrees from about 42 percent today[4] to 60 percent by 2020.[5] To achieve this ambitious goal and maintain the nation's global prominence, we must dramatically increase our numbers of college graduates.

We must help more students not only make it into college but also graduate. This critical juncture gives us an opportunity to think more deeply about how best to serve all types of students along the continuum, not just in college and graduate school but from pre-kindergarten (pre-K) to high school.

Differences in college-going rates between racial and socioeconomic groups certainly persist, but many more students of all backgrounds have access to higher education today, with two-thirds of high school graduates entering college immediately.[6] However, too few students succeed once they arrive on our campuses. In fact, nearly half of all students who begin college do not graduate, and those from less advantaged backgrounds are particularly likely to leave college without a degree. By age twenty-four, more than 80 percent of Americans born into the upper income quartile hold four-year college degrees, but less than 10 percent of those in the lowest income quartile do.[7]

Finances certainly play a role in the disparate achievement that we see. About 36 percent of undergraduates—almost nine million students—receive Pell Grants for the lowest-income families, and those grants do not come close to covering the cost of tuition at a four-year university.[8] The proportion of needy students has been increasing, from 25 percent of undergraduates in 2007–8 to 36 percent in 2012–13. However, as important as financing is, poor academic preparation plays the largest role in whether students leave college without a degree. One-third of first-time students take remedial courses in their first year, with much higher percentages of low-income and minority students doing so.[9] If students arrive unprepared in general, they are even less prepared for study in the STEM disciplines that are so critical to our country's continued economic success.

The National Academies committee on underrepresentation in science and engineering that I chaired found that by age twenty-four, only 6 percent of Americans have earned a first degree in science and engineering, compared to almost double that in Europe and even higher percentages in several countries in Asia and other parts of the world. For minority groups in the United States, the figure is only 2 percent. And so the vast majority of Americans are left out of a whole host of careers and possibilities.[10] Likewise, the US Bureau of Labor Statistics estimates that information technology will grow rapidly, adding 1.4 million job openings by 2020.[11] The only way we are going to be able to fill those jobs is to have more women and people of color getting the training they need.

In short, Americans must do much more to ensure that students not only make it into college but arrive prepared to succeed. Educators at all levels must also develop a better understanding of who their students are. We must understand their cultural expectations, ambitions, and unique strengths. We must also understand that a student's background is not her destiny. Too often, we see deficits—the negative impacts of impoverished home lives or inadequate schooling—when we should instead see the strength that students have developed from facing adversity and persevering. Changing our perception and our very culture is an essential part of the work of building a stronger educational system in which all students succeed.

As a college president, I am as interested in challenges facing pre-K education as I am in doctoral education. In *The Social Animal,* David Brooks makes the point that we are all products of our childhood experiences. Often, what appear to be careful, rational decisions are actually responses or habits we developed at twelve, eight, or even four years old. As I have shared, my life and career were profoundly shaped by my childhood experiences in the civil rights movement, and by the values and support of my immediate family as well as the community that surrounded me. Those personal experiences and my four decades as an educator have convinced me that preparing students for college begins before kindergarten. It is critical that we educators understand how strong education must be across the continuum. What we do for children in the early years will have a direct impact on what happens in middle school, high school, college, and beyond. Importantly, the reading, math, and thinking skills that young people develop in the early years lay the foundation for high-level analysis and problem solving as time goes on. Equally important, teachers and other educators play a critical role in helping students develop a sense of self. Helping a student do so at a young age can make a big difference in that young person's capacity to continue to grow and envision the breadth of his or her possibilities.

Sometimes leaders and faculty in higher education think that the work we do is more complicated than that of our colleagues in elementary school. Yet as simple as the concepts taught in elementary education might seem on the surface, we as a country are still struggling with how to ensure that every child learns to read and do math—and to love both. That struggle and the challenge of increasing college graduation rates are inextricably linked. The graduates of the nation's K–12 schools become our college students. Moreover, the teachers in our schools come out of our universities. Those teachers' ability to understand the challenges that children face and to tackle problems having to do with discipline, low expectations, and mediocrity depends heavily on universities working directly with schools, teachers, and families. Substantive progress will happen only when we move beyond what is in books and build strong relationships across the continuum.

At UMBC, we have learned important lessons from more than twenty years of experimentation in teaching and learning that apply across all education levels. For us, one fundamental lesson set the stage for all the others:

improving educational outcomes starts with changing attitudes and our very culture. We believe that culture manifests itself in every aspect of daily life on the campus. It is reflected in the questions we ask (and those we don't ask), the achievements we measure and highlight (and those we ignore), and the initiatives we support (or don't support). Changing our institutional cultures is critical to improving educational outcomes and addressing society's most pressing problems.

How can we change our fundamental attitudes about who can succeed—and at what? One way is to embrace struggle. We must teach children that not grasping a concept right away is not the same as being "bad" at a particular subject. The most brilliant of minds struggle with problems. This is the essence of innovation and even the human condition. However, people in different cultures tend to frame struggle differently, and Western cultures too often equate struggle with weakness. Likewise, researchers have found that Western teaching styles tend to associate struggle with low ability, while Eastern ones tend to treat struggle as a more normal part of the learning process. Eastern educators and students are much more likely to see struggle as an opportunity to prove oneself, to persevere. A prominent researcher in this area, James W. Stigler, recently told National Public Radio, "In America, people who are smart don't struggle, they just naturally get it. That's our folk theory."[12]

The consequences for education are clear: kids in Western cultures aren't inclined (or encouraged) to tolerate struggle, because it supposedly signals that they're not smart enough. But if the educational culture shifted and started to respect struggle and see it as necessary for advancing knowledge, then students would more easily accept it. Young people would become more comfortable with the notion that they may be "good" at math and science even as they struggle—they might even come to understand that their ability to struggle is part of what makes them a talented problem-solver.

I use the cats-and-dogs word problem precisely because the answer is not readily available, and people— even longtime educators—have to think about it. The first answer they come up with is often wrong. I am most impressed with the young people and adults who continue to work through the problem and e-mail me weeks or months later with the answer. We must help more Americans, especially our children, understand that struggle is not a sign of low aptitude. For example, not understanding algebra when first exposed to it is not the same as being bad at mathematics. Changing our attitudes on this issue is key to opening a wider range of opportunities for all Americans.

Accepting struggle is just one of the attitudes we should encourage students to adopt in order for them to be well prepared to excel later on. Here are important factors in whether high school and college students succeed:

- Being willing to take advice

- Listening carefully

- Disagreeing respectfully and attempting to understand other people's point of view

- Handling constructive criticism well

- Persevering

- Having "fire in the belly"

- Admitting when you don't know or understand something and seeking help

Perseverance is especially critical. It's not always the child who grasps the concept most quickly who will ultimately be the most successful. It is the student who is willing to struggle with the problem, who wants to ask questions about that problem, who keeps working hard at it. It is the student who looks for patterns, whether in a problem or in the discussion that you're having. It is the student who works well with other people. One thing that is significant about the Meyerhoff Scholars is they have this fire in the belly, and that is what I want teachers to develop in children whether they are six years old or fourteen to get them excited about the work.

I often share a quote from I. I. Rabi, the physicist and Nobel laureate. He has related the story that when he was growing up, everybody else's mother asked, "What did you learn in school today?" His mother asked, "Did you ask a good question today?" Questions, more than knowledge alone, lie at the heart of innovation. They lie at the heart of education. Teachers should be encouraging the curiosity of children; it makes such a difference. Fourth graders have curiosity. Tenth graders are cool; they're laid back. The challenge is to use left- and right-brain thinking, to be kooky if necessary, to get kids to laugh while they're doing math problems, to get them invested in the work in such a way that they can wrestle with a problem and argue about it, to help them understand that problems in math and science are a very real part of life and don't always have easy answers.

The dogs-and-cats word problem is a perfect illustration of this. To begin, dogs and cats are more concrete than x's and y's. But most important for educators to understand is that the point of the math problem is not *whether* the student can get the answer on his or her own, it is the *way* the student approaches the problem. Educators and parents can coach students to approach the problem from different angles. Consider what questions a teacher might ask a twelve-year-old as he guides her through the problem. I like this problem because it perfectly illustrates that education is not so much about getting the answer right as it is about learning how to think—and teaching children how to think. This cannot be done with a cookie-cutter approach. If you ask a group of sixth graders to solve the problem, each of them will start with a different approach. The challenge for educators is to meet children where they are, and in this, more flexibility for teachers is critical.

My mother taught eighth-grade mathematics, and she would say, "A problem that is even bigger than the math is finding a way to connect to students in such a way that you can pull them into the work." There is probably no time in a person's life that is more challenging and difficult than the teenage years. And we have to empower teachers to set high expectations but also meet students at their level. For example, parents and teachers alike can teach fractions with money or through cooking, such as walking a child through cutting an apple. You take an apple, show the child, and then cut it in two. Then you say, "What is this? It's half this apple. It's one out of how many parts? One out of two. That's one-half." You can do the same thing with change. "How many quarters are in a dollar? Four. So, if I have two quarters, how much of a dollar is that? Half." There are plenty of activities that will capture a child's attention and demonstrate mathematical concepts.

One of my mentees regularly brought his sixth-grade boys and girls from an inner-city school to UMBC basketball games. They could attend if they worked hard and were cooperative that week. The students saw it as a pure treat. What they did not know was that their teacher would always come up with five math problems involving the basketball game. I sat with them one game, and it was fascinating. The whole game, he and I were teaching the students probability, we were teaching them the area of different parts of the court, we were looking at the pace at which the players were moving down the court, we were looking at the number of foul shots and the likelihood a given player would make one. It was amazing to see the children get into the math, even as they were paying attention to the art of the game and which team was winning.

Using language and experiences that reflect what children already care about can make all the difference in the world.

Thus, educators must understand the developmental stages of children, along with the opportunities and challenges that come with different cultural backgrounds and family situations. Teachers face the difficult task of accounting for the very real problems that some students face in their homes, while also ensuring those same students are moving ahead academically. They must manage the classroom in such a way that all students move ahead, while each student's unique circumstances are considered. The fundamental question is this: how do we pull the students into the work?

We need to create environments where students, from elementary school through graduate school, learn how to support one another. We need environments where teachers encourage community, collaboration, and group problem-solving. Ultimately, this is the work of creating a community of learners.

If four students in a course in organic chemistry are working together, and three of them end up getting As on the midterm and one gets a C, ideally, they would all be concerned about that. The situation presents an opportunity for all of the students, even those who earned As, to improve their approach to the work. They should consider how they can learn from the person who earned a C. What is it the person did not do? Was the student's foundation in the subject not strong enough? Did the student not spend enough time alone reinforcing concepts discussed in the group? More than that, though, the students should care because people are not in careers solely for themselves but to help others succeed as well. For example, students need to understand that if they are in laboratories years from now the work will be about much more than their individual success. They will want to see their lab partners and student assistants succeeding also. The fundamental values of our university are rooted in this idea. We honestly believe universities are stronger and people grow more when they are as concerned about the well-being of others as they are about their own.

I know that this is counterintuitive to the way most

Americans think. But when you get people to take ownership of each other and to understand that a group truly
is only as strong as the weakest link, people will want everybody to rise up. We have to help students understand
that their accomplishments aren't diminished when they
help somebody else master the same material. However,
our institutional culture of grading on a curve works
against that. When you grade on the curve, you discour-
age students from working together before a test. Unless
there is a great deal of trust, I won't help Theresa, because
I am not confident that she is going to share her knowledge with me. If Theresa holds back, yet I tell her what
I know, I am going to get a lower grade. The culture in
science and math in our country tends to be just that way,
and the higher up you go, the more cutthroat it becomes.

If we are to succeed as a nation, we can no longer afford to have winners and losers in education. We cannot
afford the false dichotomies of Americans who are simply good at math and science and those who are not, of
students who just get it and those who struggle, of young
people with strong backgrounds and those with weak
ones. The reality is far more nuanced. Embracing the nu-
ance, however, strikes at the very core of our institutional
cultures. Just look at the language of higher education.
From "weed-out courses" to "grading on a curve," our
structural concepts say that not all of our students—who
have met our admissions standards, by the way—will
succeed, much less excel. It's a language that pits faculty against students and students against one another,
rather than creating a community of learners. We have to
change that thinking. To do so, educational institutions

must seriously examine their culture, asking what practices are truly essential for excellence and student success
and which are simply habit.

LOOKING UPSTREAM:
COMMUNITY COLLEGES AND K-12 EDUCATION

Partners, especially those in education, can provide useful perspective on an institution's culture. At UMBC, for
example, community colleges and elementary and high
schools help us look at ourselves through a fresh lens.
Moreover, those partnerships enable people across the education continuum to learn from one another. At UMBC
we take our partnerships with community colleges, high
schools, and elementary schools very seriously. A key ele-
ment of making these partnerships work is changing the
reward structure to create support and incentives for faculty to engage with other institutions. A willingness to
examine and, when necessary, change institutional cultures and a deep commitment to data analysis, high standards, and experimentation are essential aspects of these
partnerships.

Partnerships with Community Colleges

UMBC has partnered with four Maryland community
colleges to improve STEM outcomes for students transferring to UMBC. The work began several years ago when
my colleagues were examining student success and failure
in the STEM fields and were looking at what factors beyond race and gender impacted success. Immediately they
saw that transfer students did not perform as well as those

who started at the university as freshmen. In fact, the difference in retention and graduation in the STEM fields was striking. UMBC had long had agreements in place with community colleges to bring our coursework into alignment, and the transfer students' GPAs indicated they should be able to do the work. But the data clearly said that something was going wrong. We listened to the data, and we shared it with a number of our community college partners, including Anne Arundel Community College, the Community College of Baltimore County, Howard Community College, and Montgomery College.

The early indications were that despite the course alignment on paper, our faculty often emphasized different foundational concepts than did the faculty at our community college partners. Moreover, UMBC's culture was quite different from that of the colleges from which the students were transferring, and students often found the campus overwhelming and our processes bureaucratic and difficult to navigate. Given this situation, it would have been easy enough for us to justify continuing to do what we had always done, in the name of academic standards and consistency in our student services. We could have said that the students needed to adjust and that some attrition was only natural. Instead, we decided to take a hard look at how we could change. What aspects of our curriculum and our practices were truly an essential part of the educational experience, and what aspects were simply routine? What things could we modify in order to provide transfer students with a more seamless transition to a more welcoming university?

We formed an official partnership with the four two-year colleges on the Transfer STEM Initiative, or t-STEM, and won a grant from the Bill and Melinda Gates Foundation to support the project. We are actively working now to better align STEM curricula, learning outcomes, and competencies among the colleges, thus reducing lost credits and the need for students to retake courses. The group of colleges is working to improve academic and career advising; encourage students, faculty, and advisors to use online tools, such as an academic portfolio we are developing specifically for STEM students; and create peer-mentoring networks and transfer seminars to better support students during the transition from a two-year to four-year college. Ultimately, we aim to develop a robust "Transfer STEM Scholar Pathway" that lays out a clear program of study for each discipline, from community college to university to graduation.

The work is focused on high-impact, relatively low-cost interventions that can be scaled to reach the broadest number of transfer students possible, with the goal of ensuring that all students have the tools and support they need to succeed. Our guiding principle is that two- and four-year institutions share responsibility for the success of transfer students.

That shared responsibility extends to the K–12 system, where the country has a much greater ability and responsibility to change how students (and their teachers) see themselves in relation to STEM disciplines.

Choice Program

This program, now led by LaMar Davis, has served twenty thousand children since its inception. It seeks to alter the life trajectories of these youth by providing them supervision and mentoring and keeping them in school and out of trouble. As LaMar recently noted in an op-ed, there is no quick fix for addressing the challenges these troubled youth face. He wrote, "We need a collective approach that shifts away from isolated interventions and invests in strategies that align multiple systems in an effort to solve these complex problems." The Choice Program has been funded by the Maryland Department of Juvenile Services, and the Marguerite Casey Foundation has provided major grants to support efforts to empower families in advocating for their children.[13]

At UMBC, concurrent with our support of hundreds of high-achieving minority college students in the Meyerhoff Program, we have worked with a much younger group of at-risk youth in the Choice Program, which was started in 1987 by Mark Shriver and John Martello through the Shriver Center at UMBC (named for Mark's parents, Sargent and Eunice Kennedy Shriver). UMBC students work with the children and teenagers in their schools and regularly check in with them and their families by phone and in person on evenings and weekends. These check-ins and home visits are especially critical. For example, they ensure that the youths are staying home at night and doing homework or other productive afterschool activities. UMBC students and staff can provide accountability that parents, many of whom work at night, often cannot. Additionally, a substantial number of these children and teenagers live in homes where their parent or other guardian is struggling with drug addiction or other serious problems that limit their ability to provide support and accountability. The youths, mostly African American boys from the inner city, also attend regular after-school programming at UMBC. For many of them, their first trip to campus is not only their first experience at a college but also the first time they have ventured outside their neighborhoods. Youth who enter the program typically fall into one of two categories: some are in the juvenile justice system as first-time criminal offenders, and others come from households where drug use and other factors have put them at high risk.

What we have learned from working with these boys over the past twenty-five years is similar to lessons learned in the Meyerhoff Program and with other African American men on campus. Key lessons include the value of and need for (1) teaching young boys and young men to listen to and analyze the advice they receive; (2) encouraging them to think critically and ask questions that can help them better understand people, situations, and the problems they face; (3) helping them avoid thinking of themselves as victims and instead to feel empowered to take ownership of their future; (4) working with students to identify their assets; and (5) helping them recognize their ability to manage their own lives despite all kinds of problems. Giving African American students opportunities to write a rap song, for example, and to present their thoughts about important messages expressed through rhythm can be both inspiring and instructive.

The most important lesson we have learned through working with these different populations—high-achieving black men or first-time offenders—is that we must take an approach that is strengths-based. We are constantly helping students to identify and understand the assets they bring to the campus—from the resilience born of their life experience, to their determination to succeed. Rather than allowing students to dwell on deficiencies in their academic preparation or other obstacles to their success, we help them focus on the qualities, skills, and practices they've used to overcome obstacles in the past. We can be supportive by letting students know how much we care, while also setting high expectations; by constantly emphasizing how much we believe in them, while also emphasizing the importance of hard work, personal initiative, and respect for authority; and by helping them develop a sense of self and a vision for their future.

K–12 STEM TEACHING

A second example of culture change and partnership between universities and K–12 schools is Maryland's Project Lead the Way (PLTW) program, led by Anne Spence, an accomplished engineering professor at UMBC. The program is a national model for training middle school and high school teachers to better prepare students for college-level work in the STEM fields, particularly engineering. More than just training, though, the program works to shift the culture of STEM education at UMBC and in middle and high schools. Maryland's project is a national model, in large part because of the close and productive working relationship between the State Department of Education, UMBC, the schools, and industry partners. For example, Lockheed Martin and Northrop Grumman both provide mentors and send teams of engineers to work with students.

Each summer, as part of PLTW, UMBC hosts hundreds of teachers for training in pre-engineering and other STEM fields, and the campus also serves as a support system and hub for teachers throughout the year.

For a number of years, PTLW worked in concert with a Math and Science Partnership program, funded by a National Science Foundation grant. The Math and Science initiative trained dozens of new STEM teachers for Baltimore County middle and high schools. Many of the participants were seasoned professionals in the STEM fields interested in moving into teaching, while others were new teachers on a more traditional path. The partnership focused on identifying new research-based practices in STEM education and extending existing best practices.

A set of core elements for strengthening secondary education emerged from the Math and Science Partnership, and we continue to embrace those with Project Lead the Way. The core elements are these:

- Building strong support systems for teachers

- Emphasizing performance-based instruction and assessment for K–12 students and teachers

- Developing data-driven strategies for comprehensive school improvement in STEM areas

- Performing research to develop innovative, effective teaching practices

- Developing teaching and learning based on inquiry, solving problems, and addressing real-life issues

- Utilizing technology to enhance instruction and assessment

- Using the "5E" model (engage, explore, explain, extend, and evaluate) for STEM

- Building a teacher-leadership model that builds capacity within individual schools and across a district

- Developing culturally responsive pedagogy

The story of "Maggie," a petite biology teacher who participated in the Math and Science Partnership program, illustrates key points, particularly the importance of support systems and a culturally responsive approach to teaching. Maggie had enjoyed her time tutoring basketball players at James Madison University, and she felt that her calling was to be a great teacher in inner-city schools. Maggie could usually control her class, but she confessed that her greatest fear was that a fight would break out and she would have to run for help, losing her students' respect. One day, she announced, "I got my street cred today." Two large male students had started a fight in one of her classes. Rather than run, she pointed to two other students she had previously asked to assist her if such a situation arose. They helped her calm the fighting students, as she stepped between them and said emphatically, "You will not do this in my class."

Maggie had a plan. She had confronted her fear, and her peers in the program had helped her come up with a strategy for dealing with it. One of the real strengths of the Math and Science Partnership is that it recognized the importance not only of professional development but also of giving teachers the support they need as they work with students who have troubled backgrounds. The program created a space where it was comfortable to discuss the challenges of teaching students who have major distractions in their home life or have poor attitudes about being smart and applying themselves.

Expanding this kind of work will truly require cultural change; at universities, we can create support and incentives for faculty to engage with K–12 schools. For example, at UMBC, we have been working to retool the annual process for reviewing faculty to add a section on K–12 activities, a way of valuing and assessing the work faculty are doing in this area. This review is the basis for rewarding faculty financially and with course buyouts to allow time for engaging the schools. Moreover, programs such as Project Lead the Way and the Math and Science Partnership require culture change at participating schools, which must allow teachers the time to step back, reflect, and experiment.

We recently began a partnership with Lakeland Elementary School in southwest Baltimore that builds on lessons from Project Lead the Way and our successful Sherman STEM Teacher Scholars Program. The Sherman program, generously funded at UMBC by George and Betsy Sherman, recruits students to UMBC who are interested in majoring in the STEM fields and in teaching math and science in high-needs schools upon graduation. It provides students with a scholarship and, just as important, with peer networks, mentoring, academic support, and professional development. The foundation of the program is our pool of talented students who possess a desire to teach in high-needs schools, especially those in urban areas, and a commitment to quality education for all children.

Those scholars, along with a number of other UMBC

students and staff, are now working especially closely with Lakeland Elementary to develop family-centered strategies that address student needs through after-school and summer programming. In particular, the partnership aims to help Lakeland improve students' reading and math test scores, and it was awarded a grant from the Maryland State Department of Education to do just that. This work represents the best of partnership in that the teachers, administrators, and university faculty and staff involved truly listen to one another. It is important for those of us at UMBC to remember that teachers and administrators in elementary schools know children in ways that people at universities usually do not.

Through this program and others, we have learned that schools play a key role in helping parents develop a vision for their children that includes success—highlighting one very important aspect of community support for kids. Specifically, schools can help parents do the following:

- Realize they are already experts on their own children. They know their children's strengths, weaknesses, and interests better than anyone else.

- Understand the significance of their role as advocates for their children, both in standing up for their children and holding them accountable.

- Identify the skills and knowledge that children are expected to acquire during the year.

- Understand that academic ability is far from the only attribute that affects kids' academic performance. For example, a student may not be performing well because he or she wants to be seen as "cool" and not a "nerd."

- Connect with other parents and resources in their community.

- Identify parenting workshops that focus on helping parents understand how important their daily actions are, including reading to their children at an early age, helping their children connect numbers and word problems to real-life situations, and encouraging their children's curiosity.

As schools look to support parents, the principals, teachers, and counselors should be aware that we find examples of successful parenting in many different types of family structures: two parents or one, parents with college or graduate degrees and those with a high school education, families with two or more income earners and those with none. For our previous books, *Beating the Odds* and *Overcoming the Odds*, my coauthors and I talked extensively to dozens of parents of students in the Meyerhoff Program. Over the intervening years, I have had hundreds of sessions with other parents—from all walks of life. One thing is clear in all those discussions: no matter their education level or financial resources, parents who care and who engage their children can raise them to be curious and academically successful. Children can learn a tremendous amount by having to explain concepts— so parents who do not understand something should not be shy to ask. If you are that parent, have the child walk you through the problem. If they are uncertain of a concept, have them explain what they do not understand, and help them shape questions for their teachers. Google ideas and concepts and learn together. Again, the point is to focus on assets—the unique strengths of the family situation, rather than what it lacks. The critical ingredient is active parental involvement in the child's life—loving, encouraging, challenging, and supporting the child as the number one priority. We must ensure that our communities—and the culture in our schools—recognize this fundamental truth.

Common Core

UMBC's experience with Lakeland Elementary has demonstrated how critical it is to listen and truly work as partners, and nowhere has that been more important than in our work with elementary school teachers on strategies for ensuring that students gain the core skills needed for success. UMBC faculty and staff have worked with the schools' teachers to prepare students to be successful as they proceed along the educational pathway and—some of them—into careers in STEM. One key program has been to assist in their preparation for the implementation of the Common Core standards, developed by a consortium of state commissioners for education and governors across the country starting in 2009. The Common Core standards are designed to foster more challenging, writing-intensive curricula with more consistent learning outcomes across states, and most states have signed on to the initiative. Our interest in this initiative stems from the importance of students' acquiring the necessary skills in the classes and at the grade levels where they are taught, given how easy it is for students to fall behind and the grave consequences when they do.

The Common Core standards focus extensively on giving students foundational math and reading skills, as well as the skills to communicate clearly and effectively. Examples of standards that are particularly promising include developing the ability to solve real-life problems using numerical and algebraic equations; working with proportional relationships, developing and utilizing probability models, and defining and evaluating functions; and developing key practices, such as making sense of problems, persevering in completing problems, reasoning abstractly and quantitatively, constructing critiques, modeling with mathematics, using appropriate tools, and looking for and making use of structure.

Similarly, examples of promising standards in English and language arts include literacy in reading and writing; the ability to comprehend and evaluate complex texts; the ability to build context knowledge and to understand different perspectives and cultures through reading; facility in adapting communications to particular tasks and audiences; and the ability to understand a writer or speaker, to evaluate claims and evidence, and to offer interpretation and critique.

The standards draw on research and evidence-based best practices and will provide clarity and consistency for schools across the country as they develop guiding principles and set standards for student skills. The standards will also help parents to better understand what their children are expected to learn at each grade level. And they will provide for economies of scale in developing tests and curriculum guidelines, allowing for performance comparisons between the United States and other countries that are not currently available because of different standards across states. The standards also provide a much-needed guide for professional development for teachers and school leaders across the country. The eight states that had Common Core standards in place before the latest National Assessment of Educational Progress exams showed improvement from 2009 scores in either reading or math.[14] That is promising news.

It is true that the adoption of Common Core standards has not been without opposition. Some educators, lawmakers, and parents fear that the standards will undermine school autonomy, overly standardize curricula, and obligate teachers to adopt a particular approach to teaching and learning. However, to me, the strength of Common Core lies in the fact that strong standards are set, but great flexibility is allowed in how those standards are met. To excel, teachers must have both clear benchmarks and space to innovate. UMBC faculty and staff are drawing on past experience as we help Lakeland Elementary strike that balance.

Teacher Flexibility in Teaching Skills

In working on Maryland's Project Lead the Way, we saw firsthand that teachers did not have the time to understand what it really meant when a student was below proficiency level or to think about strategies for giving students support in building foundational skills. Moreover, they did not have the time or resources to explore how technology might help in identifying the skills the students most needed to work on and in building those proficiencies. Our current system too often forces teachers to move ahead in the curriculum even if not all of their students have grasped the foundational information key to continued success. This problem is particularly acute in mathematics and science, where each level directly builds on the one before it. It is impossible, for example, to succeed in Algebra II if you did not learn the key concepts in Algebra I. And it's impossible to grasp the concepts in Algebra I if you do not have a strong pre-algebra background.

When we think about academic innovation, we need to be giving support and resources to teachers to think creatively about how to address holes in students' foundational knowledge, even as they cover new topics required in a given course. I often hear teachers say some version of the following: "I am expected to go through topics five through nine over this next semester, but I still need to work on topics three and four. The students never got those earlier concepts or they lost that knowledge over the summer."

The Common Core standards help in setting clear expectations for mastery of skills. The question for us is this: how might school systems work with teachers to help them have more flexibility in the approaches that they take in covering material and helping students master concepts?

Currently, from primary and secondary education through postsecondary, we look too favorably on C-level work. Let's say Michael earns a C in pre-algebra. That means he understands the minimum level but doesn't have a solid grasp of the concepts. If Michael is then off for the summer or waits a semester to take the next course in the sequence, he forgets a portion of what he did know. Now Michael's understanding is at less than a C level. When he starts the next grade, the teacher will begin

with Algebra I topics, but Michael lacks a solid understanding of pre-algebra. He won't be able to follow the
lessons, and will fall further and further behind.

The question I raise for America is this: how might we
take into account—through data-driven analysis and decision making—that Michael needs to continue working
on those pre-algebra concepts, even as he begins Algebra
I? Through technology, collaboration among students,
and flexible scheduling, we should be able to develop a
system that successfully accounts for the fact that every
student is not at the same level of competence at the
beginning of a semester. Software programs and online
learning modules, for example, can help students focus
on areas in which they need to improve. Teachers can
also use clickers or other electronic devices to solicit answers from all students and to check their baseline understanding of different concepts as they advance through
the class material.

After the midterm of a course, we need to reconsider
how we work with the students who are not performing
well. A C-level performance on a midterm indicates that
a student needs to do more work before moving on to
the concepts in the second half of the course. What do
you do with the students who score a C or lower at the
midterm? Right now, we don't give teachers a chance to
do anything but continue on. Again, we need to develop
systems and tools that allow teachers to bolster students'
understanding of those first-level competencies, even
as teachers are introducing new concepts. Anyone who
knows math and science will tell you that if a student
doesn't do well in the first half of a course, the probability
that the student is going to do well in the second half is

very low. Yet in schools across the country, teachers just push ahead in an attempt to cover the material.

LOOKING AT OURSELVES: COURSE REDESIGN

We see some of the same issues in higher education. UMBC has always had talented faculty who are leading researchers in their fields. Yet year after year a substantial portion of students—particularly in math and science— were failing. And on our campus, just like on campuses across the country, the tendency was to say, "I taught it. *They* just didn't get it."

We did not understand that even if you have done a superb job presenting the material, you have not taught it effectively until the students grasp the concepts. My colleague William LaCourse understood that and got creative. Dr. LaCourse was teaching first- and second-year chemistry students at UMBC, and far too many were failing. The students, he was convinced, weren't incapable— but he also wasn't willing to accept that he wasn't a good instructor. Rather, he thought, something must be wrong with the way the course was structured, with the way the department was organizing the material. From that realization, the Chemistry Discovery Center was born. The center uses team-based, active learning to supplement more traditional teaching methods. In class sessions, students rotate through four distinct team roles—supervisor, record keeper, data collector, and disseminator—as they spend two hours each week wrestling with chemistry problems. The result? The failure rate in first-year chemistry has been cut in half, at the same time as the department has raised the standards. More students are earning As and Bs in foundational chemistry courses and, significantly, are going on to major in the field. Further, the Chemistry Discovery experience equips students with skills useful in other disciplines and in life and career, such as knowing how to work in teams, how to articulate and respectfully argue a point, and how to communicate concepts in writing.

Beyond the specifics, though, the important lesson for educators is the value of experimenting. Dr. LaCourse wasn't willing to keep failing with the same old approach—and just as importantly, he wasn't afraid to fail trying something new. That's a testament to his spirit but also to the culture at UMBC. Our experience with the Meyerhoff Program showed us the importance of taking thoughtful risks, of being bold.

Too many educators in our elementary, middle, and high schools have the drive to experiment and so clearly see the need, but they are hemmed in by processes and cultures that promote the status quo. Teachers need flexibility, support, and time to be creative about working with students of all backgrounds and all levels of prior preparation. We need to bring more innovation into the K–12 system. Teachers should be allowed to step back, to slow down if they need to in order to ensure that students are truly grasping the key concepts.

The payoff of giving educators the flexibility and support to take risks shows clearly in the impact of the Meyerhoff Program. Through bold thinking, our faculty and staff have figured out how to help students, including many African American and Hispanic students from truly underprivileged backgrounds, to not only survive in the STEM fields in college but to actually thrive. The program has been so successful that we're sending students to Harvard and MIT and Stanford for PhDs and MD-PhDs. In fact, UMBC is the leading predominantly white institution for sending African American graduates on to earn PhDs in the STEM fields.

CONCLUSION

My colleagues and I have found that, at every level of education, the key ingredients of success are fostering community, instilling a sense of purpose in students and formulating guiding principles that have student success at their center, making data-driven decisions, and taking a nuanced view of students that takes into account their backgrounds and individuality. I want to emphasize that being data-driven—looking at averages and probabilities of success—must lead to thoughtful support, not stereotyping based on students' backgrounds.

Americans, especially educators, talk a lot about K–16 these days, and yet we need better incentives for school systems and universities to form partnerships, and we need to rethink the approach we take to partnering. The programs that UMBC and its partners have developed, from the Choice Program and the Sherman STEM Teacher Scholars Program to working with specific elementary schools, have reaffirmed for us the need for students and educators to have robust discussions about goals and strategies. To the extent that the community is healthy and can engage in meaningful dialogue, people are willing to take risks to search for effective approaches. In every successful community, there will be failures; the key is to understand and embrace the lessons of those failures. It's

not the successes or failures that define us but how we respond to them. I am inspired by those who are successful
and by those who have failed and persevered. We learn
from every one on our path toward greater student success
and a stronger professional community in STEM fields.

As I said before, nowhere is the need to bring more
innovation into the K–12 system greater than in math
and science. Bob Moses—a civil rights leader, eminent
scholar, and one of my heroes—has developed a brilliant
philosophy that holds that mathematics education is
nothing short of a civil right. He has dedicated his career
to the Algebra Project, based on that conviction. "Mathematics literacy in today's information age," he has written, "is as important to educational access and citizenship
for inner city and rural poor middle and high school students as the right to vote was to political access and citizenship for sharecroppers and day laborers in Mississippi
in the 1960s."[15]

I think often about Dr. Moses's notion that we have to
find ways of bringing sensitivity to that work, of relating
math to students' lives, to their physical environments,
to things that are important to them. We need to bring
that level of creativity to mathematics in K–12 and beyond if we are to ensure that many more people of color
and women succeed.

The challenges facing our education system are ur-
gent. The only way a child in America has the possibility
of a bright future is if she learns to read and think critically. We owe every child the chance to excel. The question we must ask ourselves is, do we really believe that if
given the proper support, students from all backgrounds
and races can truly succeed? You know my answer is yes.

Afterword

I recently had the pleasure of running into Oliver Meyers on my campus. He was at UMBC to give a talk to the mechanical engineering department he had graduated from. Seeing him took me back twenty-five years to our Meyerhoff recruitment weekend in 1989. I remember a younger Oliver saying to me then that he played football, played piano in his church, and was valedictorian of his class but also that he was "from the country"—Brandywine, Maryland—and maybe that meant his schooling had not been as rigorous as that of others from schools in Maryland's metropolitan areas. He was worried that he was not as prepared as the other young men we had invited to campus that day, but he said he was sure he could build up his background and he promised to work as hard as possible in order to succeed. He did that and went on to earn bachelor's, master's, and doctorate degrees in mechanical engineering at UMBC. The day I saw him on campus, he received a letter from his university where he was on the faculty, letting him know that he had been granted tenure. Since then he has been given a tenured appointment at another research university.

This is a success story, but one with a cautionary note. While Oliver's journey at UMBC began twenty-five years ago, with his most recent faculty appointment he is the only African American on the mechanical engineering faculty there. We have come so far, yet have so far to go. We can see that this story reflects the larger landscape by looking at national data. While underrepresented minorities comprised 28 percent of the US population in 2008, they received just 17 percent of science and engineering bachelor's degrees, comprised only 9 percent of the science and engineering workforce, and earned merely 5.4 percent of science and engineering doctorates awarded by US institutions.[1] African Americans, who make up 13 percent of the US population, currently receive fewer than 2 percent of research grants awarded annually by the National Institutes of Health.[2]

We have, as a nation, achieved progress in postsecondary education. Passage of the Servicemen's Readjustment Act (the GI Bill) in 1944 provided an opportunity for veterans of World War II to attend college. Despite opposition from some academic leaders who could not imagine large numbers of lower- and middle-class GIs on their campuses, many more veterans than expected took advantage of that opportunity with significant consequences. A large number of college-educated veterans—primarily men—then entered the workforce as the postwar economy was poised to grow, helping to spur that postwar prosperity and the growth of the middle class.

This success changed the notion of who should go to college and for what purpose, permanently altering the landscape of higher education as college was more widely opened to those outside the elites for the first time.[3] The National Defense Education Act of 1958, the Higher Education Act of 1965, and the Educational Amendments of 1972 that reauthorized the Higher Education Act then combined to provide a framework for an expansive federal role in providing need-based financial aid for college students, again widening access to higher education. These pieces of legislation provided need-based grants, guaranteed and subsidized student loans, and federal work-study.[4]

Meanwhile, in 1954, the Supreme Court decision in *Brown v. Board of Education* led to the decade-long modern civil rights movement that sought to open the door of opportunity for blacks as well. The movement sought to bring down segregation, integrate public accommodations and schools, and secure the rights of blacks across the South and the nation. It was a long struggle, often met with violence, yet it secured these goals and created new opportunities for African Americans. The passage of the Civil Rights Act of 1964 was a landmark that, like the GI Bill, also significantly altered America, as the law now supported the rights of African Americans to participate fully in every aspect of our society including education.[5]

The significance of the Civil Rights Act of 1964 and the Higher Education Act of 1965 (and its reauthorizations), both enacted as part of President Lyndon Johnson's Great Society, is clear. Their impact can be seen in many places, including increased high school and postsecondary degree attainment for African Americans over the last half century. They can also be seen more broadly in other areas. For example, the percentage of African Americans living in poverty dropped twenty-three points between 1963 and 2013, from 51 percent to 28 percent. The percentage of African Americans owning their own homes increased by fourteen points, from 31 percent to 45 percent.

However, much work has yet to be done. In education key gaps persist and have even increased. The Educational Testing Service has recently noted that if you are poor, black, and male, "the odds of graduating from high school are less than 50 percent, and the chances of reading beyond the eighth-grade level, even when you graduate, are not much better." And, if black males matriculate at the postsecondary level, they still do not fare well. "The Black male graduation rate from colleges and universities is 35 percent versus 62 percent for all White students."[6] These trends are but one piece in a larger puzzle of inequality in the United States. The unemployment rate for African Americans has hovered at twice the rate for whites for the last fifty years. While incomes for African American households have risen, the gap in household income between African Americans and whites has remained largely unchanged. African American children are still much more likely than white children to live in areas of concentrated poverty, schools in many regions of the United States have resegregated since 1980, and the rate of incarceration for African American men has more than tripled from 1960 to 2010, and grown from five times to more than six times that of white men.[7] While there was much progress toward reducing inequality in the United States in the mid-twentieth century, inequality has increased significantly since the 1980s. Nobel Prize–winning economist Joseph Stiglitz has recently pointed out that the Great Recession of 2009 was particularly hard on minority households. He notes that "in the aftermath of the crisis, the typical black household had a net worth of only $5,677, a twentieth of that of a typical white household."[8]

This book, the speeches that led to it, and other speeches I have been invited to give recently, have provided me with a chance to reflect on the last fifty years, how far we have come, and how far we have left to go. Bob Meyerhoff and I never imagined the level of success we would have with the Meyerhoff Scholars Program. We are very proud that the Howard Hughes Medical Institute is now funding efforts to replicate our program at Pennsylvania State University and the University of North Carolina at Chapel Hill. I now spend as much of my time as I can traveling the country, talking about the success we have had with the Meyerhoff Program, as I did in the lectures that led to this book. I do so because "success is never final," as we say at UMBC, and by telling our stories, I can connect what we have done to people in other places who may be inspired to take on similar challenges in their own institutions. We must keep telling the stories and inspiring people's dreams, so that they too will help us tackle the much larger issues of inequality and disparity in society at large, in education, and in the STEM fields.

We must also continue to innovate. Even the Meyerhoff Program, as successful as it has been, requires continued innovation. For example, we must find ways to adapt Meyerhoff so that it can succeed on other campuses. We need to build our Meyerhoff Graduate Program at UMBC, to generate more opportunities to learn how underrepresented minority students can succeed at that level. We need to think more deeply about connecting those Meyerhoff Scholars who have graduated from UMBC and gone on to earn a PhD or MD-PhD with the career opportunities—such as the one Oliver Myers recently secured—that will allow them to be successful scientists, role models, and leaders.

When I chaired the National Academies' committee that wrote the congressionally mandated report on expanding underrepresented minority participation in STEM, we deliberately subtitled the report "America's Science and Technology at the Crossroads." We need a robust STEM workforce. We need to diversify that workforce as well. To accomplish this we must connect students to specific job opportunities. It is such a shame when African Americans who have earned a STEM degree at any level have difficulty finding a job and making progress in a career.

We need to send a clear message to the American public that students can find career opportunities with a STEM education—not only in STEM fields but in any career for which critical thinking skills are important. I am always impressed, actually, by our humanities and arts majors who take a few courses in STEM areas and are able to then successfully pursue careers in technology.

These students are broadly educated. They bring strong communication skills, they are able to put STEM work in perspective, they can think about the impact of technology on the human condition, and they can clearly explain the relevance of their work to the general public and elected officials.

We also need to address the possibilities for students in STEM at every step of the educational ladder. We need teachers in elementary and secondary schools who can not only provide quality science and mathematics education but also open students' eyes to career possibilities. At UMBC, the Sherman STEM Teachers Scholars program develops science and mathematics teachers who can do this and work with minority students in challenging schools. We also need the science and engineering community—faculty and researchers—at the postsecondary level to take responsibility for mentoring students and connecting them directly to internship and career opportunities. We now have African Americans who are placed in faculties of science and engineering departments and medical schools. We are making progress, but it is bittersweet. We are encouraged when one of our students who has recently earned the PhD becomes the first African American hire in a department, but we also need to finally, as a nation, get beyond each of these hires being "the first." We can accomplish this only by working deliberately, as a STEM community, to achieve this goal.

All of this requires culture change. Not a change in behavior alone but a change in perspective, values, and the willingness to act. Telling stories is the first step. Inspiring others is the next. Looking in the mirror comes next. Then come identifying the problem, collecting data to understand the problem, and bringing those who can enact change into the conversation and into solving and working on the problem. This is not an easy, comfortable, or brief process. It takes a community, it takes hard work, it takes time, but it can be done.

Acknowledgments

I would like to thank Theresa Perry for the invitation to speak at Simmons College in the spring of 2013 and to turn the lectures I gave there into this book. This opportunity to reflect was inspirational for me. I would like to thank Alexis Rizzuto, my editor at Beacon Press, who provided overall leadership, guidance, and editorial advice throughout the production of this book. She helped keep the writing on track, asked insightful questions about the manuscript, and provided a keen editorial eye for the text.

Elyse Ashburn, Anthony Lane, and Peter Henderson in the Office of the President at UMBC were enormously helpful to me in transforming the original lecture transcripts into a book. They researched key points, clarified the text, and wove three lectures into one manuscript. They were also helped in this effort by Karin Matchett, who edited the complete manuscript, providing clarity to both the text and the story. I would like to give special thanks to Douglas Pear who, as assistant to the president at UMBC for many years, helped me to document both key experiences in my life and the innovations at UMBC that have made this institution a special place. Doug provided the substantive background research for these lectures and, more important, provided steady support to me in my work with the wider university community.

I would also like to thank all of my UMBC colleagues and students with whom I have worked to create a campus where we strive for and achieve inclusive excellence. Without their thoughts, conversations, and hard work, we would not have succeeded in making UMBC what it is today—a national model for connecting teaching, learning, and research for students of all backgrounds.

Lastly, I would like to thank my parents, my wife, and my son for all that they have meant to me. My parents, Freeman and Maggie, first taught me the meaning of unconditional love. Jackie has been my best friend and wife for over forty years. Without her support and love, I can't imagine where I'd be today. She has always been for me a source of both wisdom and inspiration. She is the strongest person I know. My amazing son, Eric, has always had the uncanny ability to keep me humble and make me laugh at the same time. I am a better man because of him.

A Note from the Series Editor

In the spring of 2013, Dr. Freeman Hrabowski delivered the Simmons College–Beacon Press Race, Education, and Democracy Lectures, called "Standing Up for Justice, Creating Opportunity: From the Birmingham Children's Crusade to the Creation of Excellence in Science, Technology, Engineering and Math."

This book, which is based on those lectures, eloquently captures the bookends of Dr. Hrabowski's life and indeed the lives of many other African Americans who grew up in the Jim Crow South, fought with their lives to dismantle this oppressive system, and then dedicated themselves to creating opportunities for black students and other marginalized groups.

The atmosphere at Dr. Hrabowski's Boston lectures was electric, filled with a sense of anticipation and hope. Similarly in *Holding Fast to Dreams*, Dr. Hrabowski brings us a message of hope and possibility.

In describing his young life, he embodies Du Bois's mantra "Your child is wiser than you think." Dr. Hrabowski offers a moving story of what it was like to become a civil rights activist at twelve years of age. He describes the agony of his parents and their initial refusals to allow him, their only child and son, to participate in the marches. He describes how the morning following their refusal, with tears in their eyes, they gave him permission to march. Dr. Hrabowski describes the brutality he experienced during the marches and while being arrested.

We see how, as a youngster himself, he gathered the strength to support and encourage the eight- and nine-year-old children who were arrested and spent five days in jail with him. Dr. Hrabowski narrates how his family and community had prepared the children for this day, deliberately handing over to them a set of values, beliefs, and behaviors.

This book challenges us all to ask whether we are preparing today's children and youth for a life of struggle for justice. In it, as Dr. Hrabowski reflects on the fiftieth anniversary of the Birmingham Children's Crusade (in 2013), we are compelled to reflect on what we have to do in these times to educate and "raise up" the next generation. It reminds us that ours is still a new democracy, in the process of being perfected.

Holding Fast to Dreams compels us to see the connections between the struggles of the past and present, to grapple with what it means to dedicate one's life to creating opportunity for others. In this book we encounter a profoundly humane individual, who is unrelenting in his commitment to justice. The book is inspirational, uplifting, and intellectually compelling, while also providing a road map for what we must do to educate students of color for achievement in STEM disciplines. With great precision, and using both stories and data analytics, Dr. Hrabowski describes the institutional and pedagogical practices that allowed him to create a program that is the country's number-one producer of black PhDs in the sciences.

He discusses the importance of creating a culture where students work together, where an individual's success is predicated on the success of the group. He challenges notions that only some students can excel in math and science. He argues for the importance of providing students with sustained and early experience doing science, including working in laboratories, while creating among students the understanding that the development of expertise requires sustained work and careful feedback, as well as building connections with students' families.

Before the research of Claude Steele, Angela Duckworth, Carol Dweck, and Uri Treisman had become widely embraced, Dr. Hrabowski had developed a theory of practice for normalizing high achievement for black students in the STEM disciplines. He institutionalized in the Meyerhoff Scholars Program pedagogical and instructional practices that helped students develop the stamina to work hard in pursuit of a goal. Dr. Hrabowski pushed back at the dominant narrative about who can achieve, challenging the notion that "science is a gift." He created a culture of academic excellence based on the foundation of a community of students working together for the achievement of all.

Vividly and forcefully this book captures the themes

of the Race, Education, and Democracy Lectures. It instantiates the wisdom of a man—as well as his family and community—for whom education was seen as the path to freedom. In his writing and by his work, Dr. Hrabowski moves us beyond an instrumental notion of schooling. He compels us to ask, yet again, How do we educate young people to live and work in a democracy predicated on difference? This book challenges us to liberate "prestige knowledge" and make it available to all, most particularly to African American, Latino, working-class, and women students.

THERESA PERRY
Series Director
Professor of Africana Studies and Education
Simmons College
Boston

Notes

INTRODUCTION

1. Robert J. Norrell, "Caste in Steel: Jim Crow Careers in Birmingham, Alabama," *Journal of American History* 73, no. 3 (December 1986): 669–94.

2. Glenn Eskew, *But for Birmingham: The Local and National Movements in the Civil Rights Struggle* (Chapel Hill: University of North Carolina Press, 1997), notes that "African Americans earned more in Birmingham than elsewhere in the region as a result of the industrial demand for semiskilled labor" (64). While overall housing quality for African Americans in residentially segregated Birmingham was "the poorest quality housing of any metropolitan area in the Southeast" (64), one-third of black housing was owner-occupied in 1950 (63) and "in-town neighborhoods housed Birmingham's black middle-class professionals, with on average 90 percent of houses owner-occupied" (66).

3. King's "Letter from Birmingham Jail" can be found

in several published volumes as well as online. See, for example, Martin Luther King Jr., *I Have a Dream: Writings and Speeches That Changed the World*, ed. James M. Washington (New York: HarperCollins, 2003). It is also excerpted in Juan Williams, *Eyes on the Prize: America's Civil Rights Years, 1954–1965* (New York: Viking Penguin, 1987), 187–89.

4. There were more than fifty bombings and burnings between 1947 and 1953 in Birmingham, particularly in the postwar era as the racial boundaries of neighborhoods began to shift. Eskew, *But for Birmingham*, 53. See also Raymond A. Mohl, "Race and Housing in the Postwar City: An Explosive History," *Journal of the Illinois State Historical Society* 94, no. 1 (Spring 2001): 19.

5. Diane McWhorter referred to the events of 1963 in Birmingham as the "climactic battle" of the modern civil rights era. Diane McWhorter, *Carry Me Home: Birmingham, Alabama, the Climactic Battle of the Civil Rights Revolution* (New York: Simon & Schuster, 2001). Glenn Eskew has made a similar claim, writing, "The climax of the civil rights movement thus occurred in Birmingham as the ACMHR-SCLC [Alabama Christian Movement for Human Rights–Southern Christian Leadership Conference] campaign and hundreds of simultaneous national demonstrations forced a reluctant Kennedy administration to propose sweeping civil rights legislation." Kennedy himself identified Birmingham as the turning point in a June 22, 1963, meeting with civil rights leaders when he said, according to Fred Shuttlesworth, "But for Birmingham, we

would not be here today." Eskew, *But for Birmingham*, 312.

6. There are many insightful books about the civil rights movement, including Taylor Branch, *Parting the Waters: America in the King Years 1954–1963* (New York: Simon & Schuster, 1988); David Garrow, *Bearing the Cross: Martin Luther King, Jr., and the Southern Christian Leadership Conference* (New York: Vintage Books, 1986); and Juan Williams, *Eyes on the Prize*. A work more focused on Birmingham that I found very helpful both for the sweep and details of the events in that city in 1963 is Diane McWhorter, *Carry Me Home*.

7. Todd S. Purdum, *An Idea Whose Time Has Come: Two Presidents, Two Parties, and the Battle for the Civil Rights Act of 1964* (New York: Henry Holt, 2014).

8. Erika Frankenberg and Gary Orfield, eds., *The Resegregation of Suburban Schools: A Hidden Crisis of American Education* (Cambridge, MA: Harvard Education Press, 2012).

9. Suzanne Mettler, *Degrees of Inequality: How the Politics of Higher Education Sabotaged the American Dream* (New York: Basic Books, 2014).

10. In 1960 the Census Bureau asked whether the respondent had completed four years of high school or four years of college. In 1993 these questions were changed to ask whether the respondent had completed a high school diploma or GED equivalency or a bachelor's degree. National Center for Education Statistics, *Digest of Education Statistics*, 2013 Tables, Table 104.20, http://nces.ed.gov/programs/digest/2013menu_tables .asp.

CHAPTER 1

1. Zora Neale Hurston, *Their Eyes Were Watching God* (New York: Harper Perennial Modern Classics, 2006).
2. Kris Snibbe, "A Window into African-American History," *Harvard Gazette*, February 4, 2011, http://news.harvard.edu/gazette/story/2011/02/a-window-into-african-american-history/.
3. W. E. B. Du Bois, "The Talented Tenth," in Booker T. Washington et al., *The Negro Problem: A Series of Articles by Representative Negroes of Today* (New York: James Pott and Company, 1903).
4. Robert J. Norrell, *Up from History: The Life of Booker T. Washington* (Cambridge, MA: Belknap Press of Harvard University Press, 2011).
5. Many white southerners castigated Theodore Roosevelt for this dinner because the president had the audacity to have his daughter join them. Sitting with a black man, even one so distinguished, Roosevelt's critics argued, tainted the young woman thereafter (ibid., 244).
6. As Robert Norrell notes in his biography of Washington, *Up from History*, there was a strong focus at Tuskegee on producing teachers even as money from philanthropists in the North encouraged development of the school's vocational programs. "The trades emphasis . . . encouraged an identification of Tuskegee as a trade school rather than a teacher-training institution. Although it still mostly produced teachers, Washington allowed the false impression to persist to ensure continued success in his fundraising" (97).

7. Efforts to organize bus boycotts in Birmingham were not as successful as those in Montgomery, and they attracted much less attention. Diane McWhorter, *Carry Me Home*, 136.

8. Birmingham Public Library, Government Documents, "Birmingham's Population, 1880–2000," http://www .bplonline.org/resources/government/Birmingham Population.aspx.

9. Robert MacNeil, *Wordstruck: A Memoir* (New York: Penguin Books, 1990), 23–24.

10. David Brooks, a columnist for the *New York Times*, makes this point. David Brooks, *The Social Animal: The Hidden Sources of Love, Character, and Achievement* (New York: Random House, 2012).

11. *Amos 'n Andy* was a comedy set in Harlem that aired first on radio and later on television. The show was created by two white actors, who portrayed Amos and Andy on the radio. When the show was taken to television, two African American actors were hired to play the leading roles. However, the show, which featured typecast characters, was considered offensive by many in the black community and was opposed by the NAACP.

12. Wallace was well known for his support of segregationist policies, and a phrase from his January 1963 inaugural address—"Segregation now, segregation tomorrow, and segregation forever"—became a rallying cry for others sharing his views. For the "stand in the schoolhouse door" at the University of Alabama, see Garrow, *Bearing the Cross: Martin Luther King, Jr., and the Southern Christian Leadership Conference* (New

York: Vintage Books, 1986), 9, 269; and Branch, *Parting the Waters: America in the King Years 1954–1963* (New York: Simon and Schuster, 1988), 821–22.

13. Quoted in Juan Williams, *Eyes on the Prize: America's Civil Rights Years, 1954–1965* (New York: Viking Penguin, 1987), 34.

14. Taylor Branch, *The King Years: Historic Moments in the Civil Rights Movement* (New York: Simon & Schuster, 2013), covers the Montgomery bus boycott in chapter 1, the Greensboro and other sit-ins in chapter 2, and the Freedom Rides in chapters 3 and 4. Williams, *Eyes on the Prize*, covers the Montgomery bus boycott in chapter 3, the Little Rock story in chapter 4, and the sit-ins and Freedom Riders in chapter 5.

15. Branch, *Parting the Waters*, 609–12; Garrow, *Bearing the Cross*, 226; "Albany Movement," *New Georgia Encyclopedia*, http://www.georgiaencyclopedia.org/articles/history-archaeology/albany-movement.

16. For the sections of this chapter and the next on the events in the spring, summer, and fall of 1963 in Birmingham (the bus boycott, Children's Crusade, school desegregation), I have drawn on Branch, *The King Years*; Branch, *Parting the Waters*; Garrow, *Bearing the Cross*; Williams, *Eyes on the Prize*; and McWhorter, *Carry Me Home*.

17. Williams, *Eyes on the Prize*, 179–81; Garrow, *Bearing the Cross*, 227, 229; Andrew M. Manis, *A Fire You Can't Put Out: The Civil Rights Life of Birmingham's Reverend Fred Shuttlesworth* (Tuscaloosa: University of Alabama Press, 2001).

18. Branch, *Parting the Waters*, 689.

19. Williams, *Eyes on the Prize*, 181–82; Branch, *Parting*

the *Waters*, 689; Garrow, *Bearing the Cross*, 227–30; McWhorter, *Carry Me Home*, 308. Eskew, *But for Birmingham*, argues that Branch gives the SCLC leadership credit for more foresight than they actually had, that the plan was actually less tightly conceived going in to Birmingham, and that the name Project C was applied retrospectively, in April 1963 (210–12).

20. Quoted in Williams, *Eyes on the Prize*, 183, and Garrow, *Bearing the Cross*, 237.

21. McWhorter, *Carry Me Home*, 308.

22. The clergymen who wrote the letter, entitled "A Call for Unity," were Bishop C. C. J. Carpenter, Episcopal Diocese of Alabama; Bishop Coadjutor George M. Murray, Episcopal Diocese of Alabama; Auxiliary Bishop Joseph Durick, Roman Catholic Diocese of Mobile-Birmingham, Alabama; Rabbi Milton L. Grafman, Temple Emanu-El, Birmingham, Alabama; Bishop Paul Hardin, Alabama–West Florida Conference of the Methodist Church; Bishop Nolan Bailey Harmon, North Alabama Conference of the Methodist Church; Moderator Edward V. Ramage, Synod of Alabama, Presbyterian Church in the United States; and Pastor Earl Stallings, First Baptist Church, Birmingham, Alabama. See "Statement by Alabama Clergymen," available from the website of the Martin Luther King Jr. Research and Education Institute, Stanford University, http://web.stanford.edu/group/King//frequentdocs/clergy.pdf.

23. Williams, *Eyes on the Prize*, 188–89. Bevel, who had been involved in sit-ins in Nashville with the Student Nonviolent Coordinating Committee (SNCC), later joined the SCLC and initiated and led three major

SCLC projects: the 1963 Birmingham Children's Crusade, the 1965 Selma Voting Rights Movement, and the 1966 Chicago Open Housing Movement. See the *Wikipedia* entry on Bevel (http://en.wikipedia.org/wiki/James_Bevel), which draws on Randy Kryn, "James L. Bevel: The Strategist of the 1960s Civil Rights Movement," in *We Shall Overcome: The Civil Rights Movement in the United States in the 1950s and 1960s*, ed. David Garrow, vol. 2 (Brooklyn, NY: Carlson, 1989).

24. Theodore C. Sorensen, ed., *"Let the Word Go Forth": The Speeches, Statements, and Writings of John F. Kennedy, 1947–1963* (New York: Delacorte Press, 1988), 194.

25. The story of this tragic and senseless bombing is vividly portrayed in the 1997 Spike Lee film *4 Little Girls*.

26. One family had decided to have a separate service.

27. The National Academies report *Beyond Bias and Barriers* summarizes research on such biases, finding that a "substantial body of evidence establishes that most people—men and women—hold implicit biases." National Academies, *Beyond Bias and Barriers: Fulfilling the Potential of Women in Academic Science and Engineering* (Washington, DC: National Academies Press, 2007), 3.

28. Mahzarin Bahaji and Anthony G. Greenwald, *Blindspot: Hidden Biases of Good People* (New York: Delacorte Press, 2013).

29. This philosophy was consistent with that of black educators across the South who, through black teacher associations that included both teachers and principals, discussed and planned for the achievement and

development of black students. The relationships between parents and teachers in fostering education
for African American children are also consistent
with a wider approach across the South during segregation. See Vanessa Siddle Walker, *Their Highest
Potential: An African American School Community in
the Segregated South* (Chapel Hill: University of North
Carolina Press, 1996), and Vanessa Siddle Walker,
"Organized Resistance and Black Educators' Quest for
School Equality, 1878–1939," *Teachers College Record*
107, no. 3 (March 2005): 355–88.

30. Benjamin Mays, *Quotable Quotes of Benjamin E. Mays*
(New York: Vantage Press, 1983), 3.

CHAPTER 2

1. Howell S. Baum, *Brown in Baltimore: School Desegregation and the Limits of Liberalism* (Ithaca, NY: Cornell
University Press, 2010).

2. Lonnie Bunch, "An Indomitable Spirit: Autherine,"
from *A Page from Our American Story*, e-mail to the
author and others, May 2, 2014.

3. McWhorter, *Carry Me Home*, 495.

4. An unfortunate, unintended consequence of desegregation has been the loss of African American teachers, principals, band directors, and athletic directors.
Once a strong force for African American education,
African Americans are now underrepresented among
the nation's teachers and principals.

5. When the Supreme Court considered *Brown*, it also
examined four other cases. One of these focused
on school segregation in Prince William County,
Virginia. Rather than comply with court-ordered

desegregation, the Prince William Board of Supervisors eventually voted to close all of its public schools rather than integrate them. The schools remained closed from 1959 to 1964. During that time, many African American students went to live with relatives in nearby counties in order to go to school. Approximately seventy students were placed by the American Friends Service Committee with host families out of state in order to attend school. See recollections of Leslie "Skip" Griffin, a plaintiff in the Prince William case, at "Brown at 60 and Milliken at 40," June 4, 2014, *Ed Magazine*, http://www.gse.harvard.edu/news/ed/14/06/brown-60-milliken-40.

6. Freeman Hrabowski and E. F. Anderson, "Graduate School Success of Black Students from Black and White Colleges," *Journal of Higher Education* 58, no. 3 (1977).

CHAPTER 3

1. National Academies, *Rising Above the Gathering Storm: Energizing and Employing America for a Brighter Economic Future* (Washington, DC: National Academies Press, 2007).

2. In full, the America Creating Opportunities to Meaningfully Promote Excellence in Technology, Education, and Science Act of 2007.

3. National Academies, *Expanding Underrepresented Minority Participation: America's Science and Technology Talent at the Crossroads* (Washington, DC: National Academies Press, 2011).

4. Ibid., 3.

5. US Census Bureau, Educational Attainment, CPS

Historical Time Series tables, http://www.census.gov
/hhes/socdemo/education/data/cps/historical/.

6. National Science Foundation, *Women, Minorities
and Persons with Disabilities in Science and Engineering*, updated May 2014, http://www.nsf.gov/statistics
/wmpd/2013/start.cfm?CFID=9843413&CFTOKEN=
80210797&jsessionid=f030e1d19f0e14a3d8797b4e655
85f647467.

7. University of California, Los Angeles, Higher Educa-
tion Research Institute, *Degrees of Success: Bachelor's
Degree Completion Rates Among Initial STEM Majors*,
Research Brief, January 2010, http://www.heri.ucla
.edu/nih/downloads/2010%20-%20Hurtado,%20
Eagan,%20Chang%20-%20Degrees%20of%20
Success.pdf.

8. National Center for Education Statistics, Table 306,
"Degree-Granting Institutions, by Control and Level
of Institution," http://nces.ed.gov/programs/digest/d12
/tables/dt12_306.asp.

9. University of Maryland, Baltimore County, Office of
Institutional Research.

10. For further discussion of these elements, see Freeman
A. Hrabowski III, "Moral Leadership: Promoting High
Achievement Among Minority Students in Science,"
in *University Presidents as Moral Leaders*, ed. David G.
Brown (Westport, CT: American Council on Educa-
tion/Praeger Series on Higher Education, 2006).

11. College Board, *Calculus and Community: A History
of the Emerging Scholars Program*, May 2001, https://
research.collegeboard.org/sites/default/files/publica
tions/2012/7/misc2001-1-calculus-emerging-scholars
-program.pdf.

12. Jim Collins and Jerry I. Porras, *Built to Last: Successful Habits of Visionary Companies* (New York: Harper-Collins, 2002).

13. University of California, Los Angeles, Higher Education Research Institute, *Degrees of Success.*

14. Mitchell J. Chang et al., "Considering the Impact of Racial Stigmas and Science Identity: Persistence Among Biomedical and Behavioral Science Aspirants," *Journal of Higher Education* 82, no. 5 (2011): 564–96; Sylvia Hurtado et al., "Priming the Pump or the Sieve: Institutional Contexts and URM STEM Degree Attainments," paper presented at the annual meeting of the Association for Institutional Research, New Orleans, Louisiana, 2012, http://heri.ucla.edu/nih/downloads/AIR2012HurtadoPrimingthePump.pdf.

15. Kenneth I. Maton and Freeman A. Hrabowski III, "Increasing the Number of African American PhDs in the Sciences and Engineering: A Strengths-Based Approach," *American Psychologist* 59, no. 6 (2004): 548.

16. Ibid., 547. See Jerilee Grandy, "Persistence in Science of High-Ability Minority Students: Results of a Longitudinal Study," *Journal of Higher Education* 69, no. 6 (November–December 1998): 589–620; and Leonard Ramist, Charles Lewis, and Laura McCamley-Jenkins, *Student Group Differences in Predicting College Grades: Sex, Language, and Ethnic Groups* (New York: College Examination Board, 1994), https://research.collegeboard.org/sites/default/files/publications/2012/7/researchreport-1993-1-student-group-differences-predicting-college-grades.pdf.

17. Ibid., 547–48. See also Walter R. Allen, "The Color of Success: African-American College Student Outcomes at Predominantly White and Historically Black Public Colleges and Universities," *Harvard Educational Review* 62, no. 1 (Spring 1992): 26–45; William Bowen and Derek Bok, *The Shape of the River: Long-Term Consequences of Considering Race in College and University Admissions* (Princeton, NJ: Princeton University Press, 1998); Patricia Gandara and Julie Maxwell-Jolly, *Priming the Pump: Strategies for Increasing the Achievement of Underrepresented Minority Undergraduates* (New York: College Board, 1999); Grandy, "Persistence"; Michael Nettles, ed., *Toward Black Undergraduate Student Equality in American Higher Education* (New York: Greenwood Press, 1988); Elaine Seymour and Nancy J. Hewitt, *Talking About Leaving: Why Undergraduates Leave the Sciences* (Boulder, CO: Westview Press, 1997); and Reginald Wilson, "Barriers to Minority Success in College Science, Mathematics, and Engineering Programs," in *Access Denied: Race, Ethnicity, and the Scientific Enterprise*, ed. George Campbell, Ronni Denes, and Catherine Morrison (New York: Oxford University Press, 2000), 193–206.

18. In the second year, funding from the Meyerhoffs provided support to male students in the program, and funding from the National Aeronautics and Space Administration supported female students. Over the years, the program has also been supported by the Atlantic Philanthropies, the National Science Foundation, the National Institutes of Health, the US Department of Energy, the National Security Agency,

private companies, private donors, and UMBC. The Alfred P. Sloan Foundation provided funding that supported both the internship and postgraduation components of the program and program evaluation. The National Institutes of Health provided funding from several sources. The National Institute of General Medical Sciences provided support through the Minority Access to Research Careers program, and the National Institute for Biomedical Imaging and Bioengineering and the National Institute for Drug Abuse provided support for students in fields related to their specific missions. The National Security Agency support has been focused on students in mathematics and other majors of interest to the agency.

19. Freeman A. Hrabowski III and Kenneth Maton, "Beating the Odds: Successful Strategies to Increase African American Male Participation in Science," in *Black American Males in Higher Education: Diminishing Proportions*, ed. Henry F. Frierson, Willie Pearson, and James H. Wyche (Bingley, UK: Emerald Group, 2009), 207–28.

20. Ibid.

21. The key elements of the Meyerhoff Program have been outlined in many of our publications, including Maton and Hrabowski, "Increasing the Number of African American PhDs"; Freeman A. Hrabowski III et al., "Enhancing the Number of African Americans Who Pursue STEM PhDs: Meyerhoff Scholarship Program Outcomes, Processes, and Individual Predictors," *Journal of Women and Minorities in Science and Engineering* 15, no. 1 (2009): 15–37; Hrabowski and Maton, "Beating the Odds"; and Kenneth I. Maton et

al., "The Meyerhoff Scholars Program: A Strengths-Based, Institution-Wide Approach to Increasing Diversity in Science, Technology, Engineering, and Mathematics," Mt. Sinai Journal of Medicine 79, no. 5 (September 2012): 610–23.

22. Hrabowski and Maton, "Beating the Odds," 216.

23. Willie Pearson Jr. and Freeman A. Hrabowski III, "Recruiting and Retaining Talented African American Males in College Science and Engineering," Journal of College Science Teaching 22, no. 4 (1993): 234–38.

24. Freeman A. Hrabowski III, Geoffrey Greif, and Kenneth Maton, Beating the Odds: Raising Academically Successful African American Males (New York: Oxford University Press, 1998); Freeman A. Hrabowski III, Geoffrey Greif, Kenneth Maton, and Monica Greene, Overcoming the Odds: Raising Academically Successful African American Young Women (New York: Oxford University Press, 2002).

25. These studies include Pearson and Hrabowski, "Recruiting and Retaining Talented African American Males in College Science and Engineering"; Freeman A. Hrabowski III and Kenneth I. Maton, "Enhancing the Success of African-American Students in the Sciences: Freshman Year Outcomes," School Science and Mathematics 95, no. 1 (January 1995): 19–27; Freeman A. Hrabowski III, Kenneth I. Maton, and Charles M. Woolston, "The Recruitment and Retention of Talented African Americans in Science: The Role of Mentoring," in Diversity in Higher Education, ed. H. T. Frierson Jr. (Greenwich, CT: JAI Press, 1997), 103–14; Freeman A. Hrabowski III et al., "Preparing the Way: A Qualitative Study

of High-Achieving African American Males and the Role of the Family," *American Journal of Community Psychology* 26, no. 4 (August 1998): 639–68; Freeman A. Hrabowski III et al., "African-American College Students Excelling in the Sciences: College and Post-College Outcomes in the Meyerhoff Scholars Program," *Journal of Research in Science Teaching* 37, no. 7 (2000): 629–54; Hrabowski and Maton, "Increasing the Number of African American PhDs"; Freeman A. Hrabowski III, "Fostering First-Year Success of Underrepresented Minorities," in *Challenging and Supporting the First-Year Student: A Handbook for Improving the First Year of College*, ed. John Gardner, M. Lee Upcraft, and Betsy Barefoot (San Francisco: John Wiley & Sons, 2005), 125–40; Freeman A. Hrabowski III et al., "Opening an African American STEM Program to Talented Students of All Races: Evaluation of the Meyerhoff Scholars Program, 1991–2005," in *Charting the Future of College Affirmative Action: Legal Victories, Continuing Attacks, and New Research*, ed. G. Orfield et al. (Los Angeles: Civil Rights Project at UCLA, 2007), 125–56; Freeman A. Hrabowski III et al., "Enhancing Representation, Retention and Achievement of Minority Students in Higher Education: A Social Transformation Theory of Change," in *Toward Positive Youth Development: Transforming Schools and Community Programs*, ed. M. Shinn and H. Yoshikawa (New York: Oxford University Press, 2008), 115–32; Hrabowski et al., "Enhancing the Number of African Americans Who Pursue STEM PhDs"; Hrabowski and Maton, "Beating the Odds"; Freeman A. Hrabowski III et al., "African

American Males in the Meyerhoff Scholars Program: Outcomes and Processes," in *Beyond Stock Stories and Folktales: African Americans' Paths to STEM Fields,* ed. Henry Frierson and William F. Tate (Bingley, UK: Emerald Group, 2011), 47–70; and Maton et al., "The Meyerhoff Scholars Program."

26. Maton and Hrabowski, "Increasing the Number of African American PhDs," 551.

27. Ibid., 550; Maton et al., "The Meyerhoff Scholars Program," 615–16.

28. National Science Foundation, "Baccalaureate Origins of US-Trained S&E Doctorate Recipients," National Center for Science and Engineering Statistics (NCSES) InfoBrief, NSF 13–323, April 2013, http://www.nsf.gov/statistics/infbrief/nsf13323/.

CHAPTER 4

1. The answer is a range from six to fifteen. See "UMBC Professors Solve F. Hrabowski's Favorite Math Problem," online video clip, Vimeo, http://vimeo.com/45245451.

2. "CPS Historical Time Series Table: Table A-2. Percent of People 25 Years and Over Who Have Completed High School or College, by Race, Hispanic Origin and Sex: Selected Years 1940 to 2013," US Census Bureau, accessed September 12, 2014, http://www.census.gov/hhes/socdemo/education/data/cps/historical/index.html.

3. OECD, *Education at a Glance 2014: OECD Indicators* (Paris: OECD Publishing, 2014), http://dx.doi.org/10.1787/eag-2014-en.

4. "Educational Attainment in the United States:

2013—Detailed Tables," US Census Bureau, accessed September 12, 2014, http://www.census.gov/hhes/soc demo/education/data/cps/2013/tables.html.

5. US Department of Education Press Office, "New State-by-State College Attainment Numbers Show Progress Toward 2020 Goal," US Department of Education, July 12, 2012, http://www.ed.gov/news/press-releases /new-state-state-college-attainment-numbers-show -progress-toward-2020-goal.

6. Bureau of Labor Statistics, "College Enrollment and Work Activity of 2013 High School Graduates," press release, April 22, 2014, http://www.bls.gov/news .release/hsgec.nr0.htm.

7. "Bachelor's Degree Attainment by Age 24 by Family Income Quartiles, 1970 to 2008," *Postsecondary Education Opportunity* 221 (2010): 1–16.

8. Sandy Baum and Kathleen Payea, "Trends in Student Aid 2013," *College Board* (2013): 25.

9. National Center for Education Statistics, *Digest of Education Statistics 2013*, Table 311.40, "Percentage of first-year undergraduate students who reported taking remedial education courses, by selected student and institution characteristics: 2003–04, 2007–08, and 2011–12," https://nces.ed.gov/programs/digest/d13 /tables/dt13_311.40.asp.

10. National Academies, *Expanding Underrepresented Minority Participation*.

11. National Center for Women and Information Technology, "NCWIT Fact Sheet," accessed June 2, 2014, http://www.ncwit.org/ncwit-fact-sheet.

12. Alix Spiegel, "Struggle For Smarts? How Eastern and Western Cultures Tackle Learning," *National Public*

Radio, November 12, 2012, http://www.npr.org/blogs
/health/2012/11/12/164793058/struggle-for-smarts-how
-eastern-and-western-cultures-tackle-learning.

13. LaMar Davis, "Say 'Enough' to Violence," *Baltimore Sun*, September 6, 2014.

14. "Advertisements for the Common Core," *New York Times*, editorial, November 19, 2013, http://www.nytimes.com/2013/11/20/opinion/advertisements-for-the-common-core.html.

15. Algebra Project, "Who We Are: AP Staff and Biographies: Dr. Robert P. Moses, President and Founder," http://www.algebra.org, accessed June 2, 2014.

AFTERWORD

1. National Academies, *Expanding Underrepresented Minority Participation: America's Science and Technology Talent at the Crossroads* (Washington, DC: National Academies Press, 2011), 36–37.

2. Ibid., 47.

3. Suzanne Mettler, *Degrees of Inequality: How the Politics of Higher Education Sabotaged the American Dream* (New York: Basic Books, 2014).

4. Ibid.

5. Todd S. Purdum, *An Idea Whose Time Has Come: Two Presidents, Two Parties, and the Battle for the Civil Rights Act of 1964* (New York: Henry Holt, 2014).

6. Karen Prager, "Addressing Achievement Gaps: Positioning Young Black Boys for Educational Success," *Policy Notes* 19, no. 3 (Fall 2011): 7, 10.

7. Brad Plumer, "These Ten Charts Show the Black-White Economic Gap Hasn't Budged in 50 Years," *Washington Post*, August 28, 2013, http://www.washington

post.com/blogs/wonkblog/wp/2013/08/28/these-seven
-charts-show-the-black-white-economic-gap-hasnt
-budged-in-50-years/.

8. Joseph E. Stiglitz, *The Price of Inequality: How To-day's Divided Society Endangers Our Future* (New York: W. W. Norton, 2012), 70.

Index